Billionaire Thought Models in Business

Replicate the thinking systems, mental capabilities and mindset of the Richest and Most Influential Businessmen to Earn More by Working Less

R. Stevens

© **Copyright 2019 - All rights reserved.**

The content contained within this book may not be reproduced, duplicated or transmitted without direct written permission from the author or the publisher.

Under no circumstances will any blame or legal responsibility be held against the publisher, or author, for any damages, reparation, or monetary loss due to the information contained within this book, either directly or indirectly.

Legal Notice:

This book is copyright protected. It is only for personal use. You cannot amend, distribute, sell, use, quote or paraphrase any part, or the content within this book, without the consent of the author or publisher.

Disclaimer Notice:

Please note the information contained within this document is for educational and entertainment purposes only. All effort has been executed to present accurate, up to date, reliable, complete information. No warranties of any kind are declared or implied. Readers acknowledge that the author is not engaged in the rendering of legal, financial, medical or professional advice. The content within this book has been derived from various sources. Please consult a licensed professional before attempting any techniques outlined in this book.

By reading this document, the reader agrees that under no circumstances is the author responsible for any losses, direct or indirect, that are incurred as a result of the use of information contained within this document, including, but not limited to, errors, omissions, or inaccuracies.

Hello fellow Business Leader,

You live in a stressful and fast-paced business world.

When reading, everything seems logical and clear, but when you´re at work, you tend to forget quickly and move on as usual.

You forget things, because you have to process a lot of new information every single day and you don´t actively repeat the lessons you have learned.

I have found a practical solution for you. One which doesn´t require any mental energy.

The book contains **29 mental models**. But you don´t change by just reading. Only concepts that you practice and repeat will make it to your long-term memory.

So, my advice is to print these mental models. Tape the model you want to internalize to your computer screen or on your bathroom mirror. Put the model in your eyesight so you see it daily. This will help you on your personal road to more success and to hit the next level in your business.

If you want to use the thinking models of successful billionaires:

- Go to: http://billionairethoughtmodels.businessleadershipplatform.com/

OR Scan the QR Code below

- Get the 29 models
- print the model you want to work on.
- start reading and initiate the desired change

Tip: **One model at a time.**

Enjoy the book.

R. Stevens

Business Leadership Platform

www.businessleadershipplatform.com

Table of Contents

INTRODUCTION	**9**
CHAPTER 1: INTRODUCTION TO MENTAL MODELS	**15**
Characteristics of Mental Models	17
Effects of Mental Models	19
Common Mental Models	23
The Story of Charlie Munger	29
CHAPTER 2: THE WAY YOU SEE THE WORLD	**31**
Confirmation Bias	31
Framing	35
Selective Perception	37
Ideology	39
Stoicism for Business	41
Emotional Intelligence in Business	44
Decision-Making 101	48
CHAPTER 3: THE THOUGHT PATTERNS OF SUCCESSFUL MANAGERS	**51**
Decision-Making 102	51
Mental Models for Systematized Decision-Making	55
The Common Mistakes of Beginning Leaders	57
Mental Models to Prevent Mistakes	62
Story Time	67
CHAPTER 4: SYSTEMIZE FOR PRODUCTIVITY	**73**
Systemizing Organization Processes	73
Negative Mental Models	83
CHAPTER 5: NEGOTIATION—HOW TO MAKE IT A WIN-WIN	**95**
Characteristics	96
Negotiation Skills	99
Mental Models of a Negotiation	102
Common Mistakes of Beginning Negotiators	105
The Psychological Insights of Negotiation	110
CONCLUSION	**115**
REFERENCES	**119**

Introduction

Every employee dreams of the day they will be promoted from regular member of staff to a managerial position. For most people, being stuck in one position for a long time is the most demoralizing thing to go through. However, the managerial position comes with its own share of challenges. The responsibilities of a manager—even at the lowest level—are without a doubt greater than those of a regular employee. The skills you require to be considered for a managerial position, as well as those you will have to use to succeed in your new position, call for you to attain a superior mental model.

Among other things, you will have to coordinate a team, oversee work processes, and answer to the higher-ups about the performance of your division. Make no mistake about it; management is a giant leap for any employee. Apart from learning to resist sticking it to your peers about your newfound success, you will need another skill above all else. This is the skill of decision-making. As a manager, a lot of what you will be doing will be making decisions. If you do not change your mental model from employee to manager, things could quickly turn awry for you.

The greatest adjustment you will have to make as a new manager, however, is having people answering to you. Even if you move from one managerial level to another, there will be more people answering to you that before. Every decision you make in your new job will be more important, and if you are not careful, the very prospect could create massive anxiety issues that will hinder your delivery. Anxiety can be especially debilitating because it robs from you the self-belief and confidence to deliver on your new job. This is the last thing you want to do; you were obviously promoted because your bosses saw something in you. Stagnation is the best-case scenario for people who under-deliver in junior managerial positions. Demotion happens to be the worst, and your career might never recover from that.

Another thing that new managers struggle with is doing their old job, sometimes on top of your new responsibilities. Because the old job got you your new position, it is highly likely that your mind will gravitate toward it as a safe and proven alternative to the new and unproven world of team leadership. The only problem with this is that you will not have the energy to do your new job to the best of your abilities. When you suddenly find yourself leading a team, you will be tempted to think that performing your old job will prove to your team that you are the kind of leader who leads from the front. The only problem is that you will not be leading from the front; you will be working from the front. As a manager, your leadership comes more from plotting the path that your team will follow into the future than working on the day-to-day issues.

A managerial position comes with some authority and power. For some new managers, they cannot resist using their newfound power to shove their subordinates around. Sometimes you move into your new office and have to fire someone soon thereafter for valid reasons. You should not hold back just so you do not seem to be flexing your muscles. In fact, some of the most effective managers tend to be those who make some dramatic power move soon after being promoted. However, you should avoid doing so to flex your muscles because, for one, your seniors will not appreciate that.

Another area where most new managers struggle at is in determining just how much you need to work. Does moving up the ladder mean that you can start working fewer hours, or does the increased responsibility mean that you should work weekends and give yourself over to your job? If there is one area where the phrase "Work smart, not hard" applies best, then it is in managerial positions. That is not to say that the managers who work overtime and weekends even after being promoted are doing it wrong, but often you will find that they struggle to delegate or they are trying to justify their promotion by working harder than ever. The flip side is to delegate all the paperwork and focus more on strategic planning for your division. Your bosses will always be appreciative of a manager who comes to them with a plan on how the company can optimize a certain aspect of their business. After all, that is why they promoted you in the first place; they saw some potential in you.

Whether you are in a managerial position or hoping to be promoted to one, you need to learn how to make better decisions. This means that not only should your decision-making process be optimized, but it should also result in higher-quality decisions. People tend to waste a lot of their time and energy in the decision-making process because their approach to the issues on which they need to decide is wrong.

Biases also affect decision-making and lead to the wrong decisions altogether. When you make the wrong decisions in your personal life, you will waste a few thousand dollars at most, maybe get your heart broken, or waste a few months or years of your life. When you are a manager, the wrong decision will lose the company time and resources and bring the stakeholders down on your boss. Your bosses cannot afford to have that happen, so they will usually try to weed out possible letdowns before it comes to that. The one thing you will realize about managerial positions is that there is a very tiny margin of error. One mistake and you are out, with a good recommendation letter possibly being your only consolation.

The bottom line is that you cannot afford to make mistakes when you are a manager. Every decision has to be right or at least be mostly right—a higher-quality decision. You need to approach every problem in the right perspective, be aware of all your biases, and weed out any distractions. In turn, you will get more confident, lead better, and command greater respect from subordinates and superiors alike.

In this book, we will address the issue of decision-making in positions of leadership. Our focus will be on the mental models through which managers and team leaders arrive at their decisions. Mental models inform everything—from the way managers process information to the kind of questions they ask when faced with a conundrum and the way they answer questions. If you address the mental model you use to make your decisions, then your suitability to a position of leadership will be granted. If your bosses have not seen it yet, they will soon identify you as an employee who deserves a promotion.

Nothing works better in inspiring people than the story of other people who have made it before them. In this book, we will lean heavily on the stories of successful people like Elon Musk, Jeff Bezos, Ray Dalio, Warren Buffett, Walt Disney, and Bill Gates, to name a few. These men established some of the world's most successful businesses and outdid themselves as inspirational managers leading thousands of employees. Their stories, especially how they prevailed in the face of challenges and continued to press forward even after encountering bitter failure, leave a lot to be desired and teach some very important lessons. The inspirational stories of these men will be weaved into the book as a practical guide to show you that men have achieved that which you most desire—success.

The theories on how to attain a managerial mindset or crush it in your new job as manager will be brought to you in a narrative style, infused with practical lessons from the aforementioned super achievers. In the end, you should be able to apply decision-making to enhance your work process, increase your efficiency, and get more done in less time and with fewer resources. This may sound like a pitch for some Ponzi scheme, but it is the sort of improvement possible in your professional life if you follow the mental models of Charlie Munger and Warren Buffett. These two men have managed to build an investment fund 20,000-fold in just four decades. The mental models they use will feature prominently in the first chapter of this book.

In the second chapter, we will touch on destructive mental models, including framing, confirmation bias, selective perception, and ideology. After helping you identify the negative thinking styles that have been sabotaging your decision-making, we will introduce the positive models of thinking for better decision-making. They include Bayesian thinking, reverse thinking, the Pareto principle, KISS, and the minimum viable product. Finally, we will address the one area of a managerial career where you must exercise your power—negotiations. In the end, you should be perfectly capable of moving into that new office and impressing both your subordinates and your seniors. If you are already in that office, you can adapt these lessons to improve your job performance and further your career.

Chapter 1: Introduction to Mental Models

Every one of us has our own way of looking at and understanding the world around us. These strategies of interacting with our environment are called *mental models*. They influence not just our thinking but also our perception of challenges and opportunities. A person with a positive mental model will see opportunities in challenges while others perceive hardship. In trying to understand people and their behavior, mental models can paint a very distinct picture of how their brain works. This is because each one of us uses mental models to break down complex issues. As such, everything we do can be traced back to the mental models under whose influence we did it.

Technical professionals are trained to look at the world in terms of systems while social scientists think by looking at the incentives behind every word and every action. The sciences teach us to look at the world from the perspective of evolution, while religions examine everything through the eyes of higher powers. Using any one discipline alone will leave you with a massive blind spot, which can be detrimental to effective thinking. Only by combining all existing disciplines can you form a rational and well-rounded opinion about a subject and, ultimately, make the right decision.

With mental models, we attempt to create a latticework of theories in our minds and put them together in a practical model. Mental models are formed from education, both formal and that which comes from experience. The more educated you have about a subject, the better you will be about tackling issues in that particular area. The lessons you receive on a variety of topics ultimately creates your mental model.

Another way to illustrate mental models as a latticework of lessons and experiences is the nail-and-hammer analogy. To a person who walks around with a hammer, everything looks like a nail that deserves nothing than to be thumped hard. The more diverse and flexible your mental model is, the better you will be at a varied number of things.

When you don't have a mental model to fit a situation, human psychology is such that you will torture the reality you encounter to fit into the most relevant of your models, which is rather boggling. You would think that it is easier to stretch the models you have to fit the situation rather than going the other way round, but for most people, this is not the reality. Unless you train your brain to adjust to new encounters through a *mental model*, you will invariably twist situations instead of seeing them for what they are. A perfect example is a manager who has an insecure mental model. Everything around them will be viewed as a threat, including the well-meaning employee who comes to them with an idea to improve the efficiency of the division.

Mental models come in two basic types—simple generalizations and complex theories. In most cases, a simple generalization comes from thought patterns that have not been examined or lazy thinking. Simple generalization breeds stereotypical thinking because the person would rather judge at first sight than examine something further. When someone says that people from such and such place are rude or untrustworthy, they are essentially grouping everyone into one category based on their experience with a small portion of the whole. Simple generalizations breed such flawed thinking as sexism, racism, and other forms of discrimination.

Complex theories are thinking models that are arrived at

through a process of detailed evaluation. Mental models based on complex theories include the scientific method and critical thinking, among others. Complex theories also inform our thinking and, most notably, best illustrate the nail-and-hammer principle. If you do not know how to think critically, you will use whatever mental model you have, whether complex or generalized, in situations that require critical thinking. Understanding the mental model needed in every situation is thus very important because it informs our decisions.

The most important conclusion from this is that your views on the world will affect your decisions and their outcomes. Success in your chosen career will depend, in many ways, on the mental model through which you make decisions. If you use the right model, your decisions will result in more success and money than you could ever dream of because you will be able to manage your time in a gainful manner and enhance your overall efficiency in life.

Characteristics of Mental Models

Some of the most pertinent things to keep in mind about mental models include their limitations, flexibility, and reliance on information.

Limitations

Mental models inform the way we interpret information and events around us. We usually form mental models based on our experiences or learn them from various sources, such as books or other people. A mental model covers a very minute aspect of our lives compared to the complexities that exist in it.

There are only a few areas of your life where you can apply a particular mental model. Luckily, there are just as many mental models as there are life situations. You can always find a mental model that is better suited to your specific situation within your personality. For example, if you have developed a fighter mentality and do not believe in giving up, you can always adopt a different mental model if the one you have been using to pursue a certain goal proves to be ineffective. Another limitation is that situations might come to you in such a way that all mental models you have developed do not quite cover it.

Flexibility

Luckily, mental models are usually flexible regardless of how we formed them in the first place. Mental models learned from early life experiences will often be unlearned as we go along meeting new people and learning new things. The decision to keep holding on to a mental model is one we make every day. If a mental model has been working well for you over time, it is totally expected that you will keep on holding it for as long as it continues working. This explains why Charlie Munger and Warren Buffett have held on to their mental models of value investing for such a long time.

However, when a mental model proves inefficient in a particular situation, it is entirely possible for you to adjust it. This is a healthier strategy than warping your interpretation of a situation to match your mental model. As much as you might feel like you have no fixed personality because you deviate from your chosen mental model when faced by different situations, you will make better decisions when you recognize that a one-size-fits-all mental model is not just impossible, but it is also impractical.

Reliance on Information

The decision to use one type of mental model over another relies on your ability to receive, interpret, and act on information. Mental models depend on information to develop and apply. For example, when Charlie Munger receives an investment opportunity, he must find out more about the opportunity before deciding whether it presents him with a chance for value investing. As much as we need to develop mental models, their effectiveness in streamlining our work or personal lives depends entirely on how efficiently we apply them. The only efficient way to apply a mental model is after evaluating all available information.

To become an efficient manager, you must, therefore, question every fact and every opportunity you encounter. Without proper questioning, you will never identify the opportunity that comes cloaked as a challenge or the problem that comes disguised as an opportunity. Therefore, the most reliable mental model to adopt is to question thoroughly everything that comes your way before acting.

Effects of Mental Models

Mental models affect every area of our lives. The way we view our world is as distinct to each one of us as the fingerprint. That is why one person sees an opportunity where others see a challenge. It is also why people react differently to different stimuli. In this section, we look at the effects of your worldviews on your decision-making capabilities. Specifically, we will look at how worldview affects your chances of time management, efficient work, success, and making money.

Time Management

As a manager, you will discover that a lot of the work you will be doing will be making decisions. You will also have to live with the fact that your decisions will have a greater impact on a larger number of people. As a manager, you will be part of the leadership of the company, responsible to the shareholders on financial output and business strategies. The long-term strategies that the senior management formulates will rely on the supervision of junior managers like you who are accountable for the company's grassroots. Therefore, your decisions will carry greater weight as a junior manager, and you cannot afford to make the wrong ones. This means that your worldview must be correct in every decision-making situation.

It is also for this reason that mental models are so indispensable to managers. They simplify our decision-making process by teaching us to look at specific aspects of an argument presented to us. Mental models are formed from years of experience or simply by reading about them from people who have been through a similar experience. In this book, we will teach you mental models gained from experience and critical observation of some of the world's best managers and thought leaders. By applying the correct mental model to a complex situation, you can always arrive at a quick solution and avoid spending too much time trying to disprove a theory and instead work on it. One reason why it is important to manage your time well, especially in relation to decision-making, is that you will be called on to make decisions at critical moments, like deciding whether to follow through on an opportunity. If you waste too much time deciding whether to explore an opportunity, you might wake up to find it gone.

In fact, a mental model exists for this very purpose. It is called the Occam's razor, and it posits that the simple explanation to a complex scenario is most likely to be the most accurate one. People who understand this mental model will make their decisions based on whatever explanation is the least complicated. Moreover, when the explanation does not seem to satisfy you, there is always the delayed judgment mental model. Here, you should never make decisions immediately if you can delay them to a later day. Alternatively, there is the suspended judgment in which you make your decision but still leave room for changes that might necessitate you changing it.

Efficiency

The most successful businesses are those that manage to create the most utility from limited resources. This is called efficiency, and it is critical for every part of life. However, in business, efficiency is even more important because it affects the business' ability to compete and make the maximum from minimum resources. The more effective you can make your department, the greater the profits you will be able to generate for your employer. A high ratio of output divided versus input means that you have a greater ability to make money. This increases your chances of getting a promotion into higher office up the corporate ladder.

Mental models streamline your decision-making process— meaning that the time between receiving an opportunity and the time at which you decide to either act on it or not will be lesser. Furthermore, mental models can be used to increase your effectiveness. For example, the subtraction model allows you to cut out any extras from every decision and every plan you make, increasing your efficiency. The better you are at subtracting, the more efficient you will be at cutting out the unnecessary parts of every process in your department, and the more efficient you will be overall as a manager. Interestingly, your ability to create an efficient system relies on your ability to create a system to determine the efficiency of every aspect of your work. This includes staff number, resource allocation, and collaboration, among other aspects.

Success

Your success at your new job will rely very heavily on your ability to manage time and work efficiently to deliver on the objectives you set for yourself. Your success as a manager will depend on your ability to deal with complex issues that will arise from your job day after day. If you can handle complex situations and make the best of them, then your success will be all but assured. Failure to command control will most probably leave you burdened by unwinnable situations. According to experts, the best way to command a situation is by building an effective mental model to simplify the decision-making process.

A mental model allows you to make sense of numerous data points and identify the connections between ideas that will come to you every single day at the workplace. With no definitive way of assessing all the information you receive, the sheer volume of thinking needed every day would paralyze you. But with the right mental model in every situation, you can know (just like a pilot knows how to operate the sophisticated dashboard in the cockpit and fly an airplane) how to make sense of complex information by isolating the most relevant points and acting on them.

Just like every other system, you should update your mental models to keep them current at all times. You can do this by using the models you currently possess in a fluid, deliberate, and strategic manner. By doing this, you will create a system of thinking through, which your managerial career will thrive but also one that will be self-sustaining enough to assure you of success in the long run.

Money

As much as money is associated with success, these two can exist in two different planes. When dealing with money, the only thing in question is the handling of personal finances. It is a relatively narrow field but one that is just as important, if not a little more so. Your financial endowment determines, in a huge way, your capacity to own the comforts you need to be able to do your job well. Whatever mental model you use in managing your personal finances will have a huge effect on the kind of lifestyle you can maintain over a long time and, in turn, your capacity to deliver year after year in your managerial position.

As far as mental models for money management go, the most effective is the rule of compounding. As you think about a retirement investment, compounding will grow any money you save exponentially.

Common Mental Models

As an introduction to mental models, we shall look at some of the most effective mental models out there. They include success by subtraction, the outlier algorithm, and the protégé effect.

Success by Subtraction

Success by subtraction is a mental model whereby you extricate from your life or work all the negative aspects, simplifying everything and thus being able to move ahead into greater success. This mental model has been referred to in various ways, including the "Less is more" slogan of world-renowned architect Ludwig Mies van der Rohe. In critical thinking, subtraction allows you to remove all the noise from a concept and look at the underlying idea for greater clarity. When making some strategic decision, subtraction allows you to shed off the extra baggage and improve your chances of winning. Depending on the strength of your ideas and character, you can use subtraction even in times when it might look to the world like a terrible idea.

The actions of the Arizona Women's Softball team coach in 2007 best illustrate this idea. With his team set to start participating in the Women's College World Series the next day, the star pitcher broke a team rule that warranted a suspension from the team. Most coaches and business leaders for that matter would cut their star performer some slack "for the greater good." However, Mike Candrea was cut from a different cloth, and he decided to drop her from the team. He reasoned that she was a huge distraction from the team because she had broken the rules of being a team. If he allowed her to come along by overlooking a major infraction, he would be sending a subliminal message that she was better than the team or that the team relied on her to function.

His actions boosted the team spirit and prompted each player in the team to work extra hard as they came together and annihilated the rest of the roster, including their greatest opponent, UCLA, to lift the Women's College World Series. It requires great courage and convictions to be able to do something like this. For most people, they would rather keep the wildcard in the team than take a risk on a more reliable player.

This concept applies to most things in life. Even at the workplace, sometimes it is necessary to cut off a work process that everyone has been using for ages. If by your critical evaluation something does not add to the good of the team, removing it will tilt the odds back in your favor. It is basic mathematics—two negative signs equal a positive sign, and positive and negative equate negative. Removing that which takes away from you adds to your value while leaving it in means that you will always be lacking something.

Subtraction works in every area of management. Do you want to start by outlining a list of your priorities for the team you have been appointed to lead? Subtract the priorities from ten to five, from five to three, and from three to one. With fewer priorities, you will focus your efforts on a few of the most promising goals and increase your chances of attaining them, and while you should not go around firing people, consider the story of Jack Welch, General Electric chairman and CEO from 1981 to 2001 and the man who steered the company through a growth period of about 4,000% in two decades.

When Jack Welch started at General Electric, it was an old company, staid in its ways and bloated by inefficiencies of age. Having been an employee of GE all through his career, he understood that the bureaucratic nature of its operations was discouraging to the hardworking employees. A firm believer in the concept of success by subtraction, he enforced a policy whereby he would fire every employee in the bottom 10% of every department in the company. GE improved drastically as a result.

The law of subtraction has been proven to work in other areas of life, too, because in an ineffective system, the things we spend most of our time on turn out to be the least profitable. By adopting the subtraction mental model, you will improve not just your job performance at the office but other areas of your life as well. You will dedicate your time to the most important things, improve your overall efficiency, and bring greater success to every aspect of your life. And because your personal life will always bleed into your work life, subtracting the harmful from your life will actively enhance your work life as a prospective or new manager.

The Outlier Algorithm

An outlier is a data point that varies in a significant way from other data points in a cluster. Outliers are a subjective statistical phenomenon that may result from a range of anomalous causes. However, it is a mathematically established fact that every 1 in 22 data points will be different by as much as twice the value of the standard deviation in a dataset. With a sample of 1,000 data points, the outliers could vary by as much as three times. But how exactly does this highly mathematical phenomenon apply to mental models?

People with an outlier mental model are adept at identifying the things that everyone else misses that have the best chance of bringing them success. Someone with an outlier mentality will set themselves apart from everyone else by "thinking outside the box" to come up with unique solutions to common problems, making themselves indispensable to the whole.

One of the most popular (but unsung) uses of the outlier mental model was the formation of Airbnb by roommates Brian Chesky and Joe Gebbia. The two former classmates came up with a multibillion-dollar idea by thinking outside the box and combining accommodation and residence.

By learning to look outside the box, you can improve your efficiency in solving problems, coming up with new ideas, and executing common business functions. And as usual, differentiating yourself from the crowd is granted to give you greater recognition and success in terms of career advancement and monetary rewards.

The Protégé Effect

Roman philosopher Seneca once said that people learn while they teach. This saying is as true today as it was 2,000 years ago. While you apply yourself to teaching others, you learn almost as much or more than them. This is because student teachers have to work twice as hard as their students do in order to be able to teach them. As a result, students who also tutor other students have been shown to perform significantly better than those who only study for themselves.

As you teach your coworkers the ropes of your workplace, you will automatically get better at it and post outstanding results in your own work. As an employee aspiring to one day become a manager, this is one mental model you could adopt to attract the attention of your superiors. As a young manager, you will be more effective in your job if you undertake the task of teaching new concepts you introduce to the workplace by yourself. The best thing about a protégé mindset is that it allows you to learn not just as you teach others but also from yourself. The mistakes you make in your quest for excellence will become great teachers and enable you to improve constantly upon the foundation you have established for yourself.

In a constantly changing world, information is the most effective tool for self-empowerment. Your success as a manager will rely, in a way, on your ability to learn, process, and apply new information. Similarly, your efficiency in your new position will be influenced in a huge way by your ability to learn and improve. In business, the protégé effect is best observed in mentorship. While you teach a promising new hire the ropes of making it in the job, you will improve your own ability to perform your job. What's more, mentorship is an inherently ego-inflating experience. You feel good to know that someone else is looking up to you, so you will pursue success more purposefully.

The capper on having a protégé mindset is that as you improve and move up the ladder to senior management, you will leave behind a great employee to continue the good work you started. And whether you like it or not, the performance of the department you left to take up your new position in a more senior position will be used to judge your mettle as a manager. Even the most successful CEOs will be considered less successful if the company they used to lead goes into a tailspin of poor performance after their departure. Jack Welch is one manager whose standing has taken a beating after leaving his last position because General Electric fell in market value after his exit.

Few other mental models work better than the protégé effect in inspiring personal improvement. This is because while you face competition from the peers who feel (probably quite justly) that they deserved the promotion just as much as you did, the people you mentor as part of your protégé mental model will prove to be an indispensable support network to prop your career.

The Story of Charlie Munger

Charlie Munger is currently among the most outstanding investors in America. He is the highly decorated right-hand man to the world's richest investor, Warren Buffett, at Berkshire Hathaway. However, Charlie Munger has always been his own man. Warren Buffett has been quoted asserting that Charlie has always danced to his own music. The two Omaha natives share a cordial relationship and investment strategies—a bond that makes them a very formidable team. Charlie has been working with Warren Buffett in the investment industry since the 1970s and has accumulated a fortune worth over $1 billion in the process.

What most people do not know is that he had tried his hand in investing long before Warren Buffett and Berkshire Hathaway. Between 1962 and 1975, he ran Wheeler, Munger, and Co. investing in the Pacific Coast Stock Exchange. This operation was a terrible loss-making venture. It made losses of 32% and 31% in 1974 and 1975 respectively. When he joined Berkshire Hathaway, Munger joined a company that was run on the principles of value investing. Buffett introduced him to the mental models of compounding, which enabled him to turn his investment career around and start making money, rising up the ranks to vice-chair today. A simple change in mental models was enough to turn Munger's investment career around and steer it toward profitability.

Chapter 2: The Way You See the World

As a manager, you will be responsible for the interpretation of complex information and data sets for your company. It is imperative that you interpret all the information you receive in the most accurate way possible. You must treat information as a separate entity from you and ensure that you understand the data as it is, rather than as you want it to be. This requirement for a high level of accuracy calls for a high level of awareness on the personal biases we hold that may warp our understanding of information. In this chapter, we shall look at the most common and debilitating personal biases. We shall evaluate the ways through which they affect our interpretation of evidence and how you can retrain your mind to think in the context of your corporate life.

Confirmation Bias

Confirmation bias is a phenomenon through which people select the information that confirms their own beliefs from a piece of evidence. Confirmation bias is especially common when we have invested ideologically or emotionally in a belief. In these instances, being proven wrong feels like a hit on our self-worth. Usually, people fight hardest to avoid having their self-worth invalidated. As a result, they will pick out tiny pieces of evidence from a pool of information supporting their views and hang on to them stubbornly regardless of the evidence to the contrary.

In confirmation bias, we act like financial criminals covering the paper trail to avoid being caught. We are already wrong, but instead of confronting the mistakes of our past, we gloss over it with tiny bits of truth from whatever sources we can get them. It indicates that we hold personal pride higher than truth and knowledge. The underside to confirmation bias is that it often leads to spectacular failures when we cannot recognize past wrongs and learn from them.

Warren Buffett describes confirmation bias as a human phenomenon whereby we interpret every new piece of information we receive in such a manner that any previous conclusions we have made are not challenged. But in a world where nothing is assured, change is the only thing you can count on. So to hold fast to beliefs formed in the past, even in the face of new information, is grossly erroneous. In fact, it is by being ever willing to be proven wrong that we can challenge ourselves first to vet any belief we have thoroughly before adopting it. Moreover, keep evaluating it from time to time to be sure of its validity, and finally, be flexible enough to change any time we receive evidence to the contrary.

The cost of confirmation bias in business is wrong decisions, faulty projects, and losses. As a manager, you should be aware of exactly how confirmation bias affects your personal and professional beliefs. Essentially, personal confirmation bias leads to you only looking at and accepting the information that confirms your beliefs. It makes you a poor manager but does not necessarily affect your employer—for example, your views on gun rights in an industry that has nothing to do with gun rights, veganism in a non-food industry, how much better a latte tastes with or without vanilla, or any other personal view you may hold. Even though you may be biased as far as all these subjects are concerned, your job delivery need not suffer.

Professional confirmation bias is the more serious kind of prejudice a person can hold. It creeps up on us even when we are not aware—when we are actively trying to avoid making warped decisions based on our confirmation bias. For example, when conducting research for a new product idea you may have just had (which is bound to happen among product managers eventually), confirmation bias creeps up on you even without you being aware. In the following manner, you ask your team to design a research study to find the viability of a product you honestly believe to be the next big thing, either in the company or in the whole industry.

Straight off the door, your team is biased. All the information they will gather from the public will be to confirm or rule out the viability of your idea. But (and this is where it gets even trickier) because they are biased, they will most likely present questions in such a way that the respondents give them whatever information they are looking for. They will definitely not do this intentionally because confirmation bias often exhibits in some of the most well-meaning areas like impartial studies. But the results from the study will be biased and probably lead to a loss-making decision.

To avoid this particular and very expensive confirmation bias, be sure to conduct studies in a truly neutral and impartial way. For example, instead of asking respondents whether a certain feature would be good for a product, ask them to rank the existing product features in terms of their importance, then ask for recommendations on improvement. That way, you will be asking the customers to point out what they would like in a possible product instead of shoving your idea in their face. Whatever product you make from a study of real preferences for customers is likely to be more successful than the one that you created of your own volition.

With that being said, it is important to point out that confirmation bias exists where objectivity does not. The surest way to remove any confirmation bias from a discussion and the interpretation of evidence is to take a step back and evaluate all the information neutrally. In a teamwork situation, the best way to avoid sliding into the slippery slopes of confirmation bias is to have a *devil's advocate* in your team. This role might not be very suitable for you as the manager because some employees will take your word as the gospel truth. Recruiting an outspoken person and encouraging them to speak out on every discussion—however contrarian their views might be—could save you a lot of trouble because you are more likely to spot holes and contradictions in an argument that way.

There is all the incentive for you to seek to remove any hint of confirmation bias from all your decision-making. Amazon is one company that has built its foundation on an objective analysis of market needs and then worked to present users with exactly what they need. According to Jeff Bezos, experimentation and measurement have been a part of the company's culture from its foundation. Instead of looking for evidence to support his views, Jeff uses scientific methods to measure the support for every idea raised within the company. Only if the data supports a decision does he authorize it.

Amazon was built on a foundation of giving the customer what they want. To Jeff Bezos, any sort of confirmation bias influencing his company's perception of what the customers want would be contrary to the very essence of the company. The success of Amazon and Jeff Bezos, currently the richest man on earth, was possible only because he went out of his way to remove confirmation bias from his decision-making process and give his customers exactly what they wanted.

The thing about eliminating all traces of confirmation bias is that it gives you a very distinct advantage. When you make objective decisions that you can count on to be true as many as ten years from now, you can apply yourself to its attainment even if you do not see the gains immediately. Therefore, not only does the elimination of confirmation bias improve your ability to get the correct facts, but it also empowers you to pursue goals with full confidence that you are on the right path.

Framing

Framing is the foundation of mental models through which we look at the world. In essence, framing constitutes the different pathways through which we think and the concepts we employ to communicate with each other. In thinking, framing determines the ways through which we interpret the data we receive and decode our own thoughts. In communication, framing denotes the different methodologies through which different actors send out information. Studies have shown that the power of framing is even strong enough to swing political elections. The way a candidate presents their ticket vis-à-vis their opponents could change the issues voters prioritize when making their choice of candidate, making an unlikely candidate win.

The same concept is used in marketing. Products are rarely described using their qualities. Mostly, the benefits they bring to you as the consumer will be hyped so that you see nothing but the advantages of buying. Even is a product is not the best in the market, the fact that they made you associate their brand with the benefits of whatever product you are buying could endear their product to you far above their competitors.

When communicating, framing is of utmost importance. With just a few changes to the wording, the meaning of a whole passage could be changed and made to sound very different. You can say two different things with very similar words or use very different words to say one thing. For example, in the stock market, when a share plummets in price, the word "correction" makes it more palatable and avoids the more anxious term like "plummet" or "tumbling." More ominously, depending on what source you hear it from, *genocide* could be referred to using the tamer phrase "ethnic cleansing."

It is for this reason that you should train yourself to speak articulately at all times, leaving no chances of misrepresentation of whatever you say. As a mental model, framing is a model developed through evolution to help our brains to deal with adversity. When you refer to death as a "loss," it falls into the category of lesser adversities like losing your keys, losing money, and such. It is a method of unconsciously lessening the pain that every human being invariably uses. And when used in this way, framing can be downright comforting. However, at the office, where everything needs to be clear and transparent, it might lead to misunderstandings or misrepresentation of facts.

The first rule of framing is that we get the answers to the questions we ask. And depending on the position we are on an issue, we will frame our thoughts about it in a particular way regardless of how objective we try to be. In communication, framing can best be described as "reading between the lines." Even though it does not tell you the whole story, it tells you enough to know a person's real feelings about an issue.

In thinking, framing is more deliberate. One person chooses to think of a problem as an opportunity while another looks at it as a challenge. Whichever way a problem comes, you choose to frame your thinking about it negatively or positively. Either way, you will find some supporting evidence to prop up your thinking. And when managing people as a junior manager, understanding framing can be valuable to ensure that you pay attention to cues that hint at deception among your employees.

Selective Perception

In a debate, each side is always coming up with ways to strengthen their position and convince the other side that they have it right instead of listening and attempting to come to an agreement. Just like confirmation bias, selective perception causes people to pick out the points they agree within a set of information and completely ignore the rest of it. Any information that contradicts your particular view is usually dismissed without a second thought, while you dwell on that which is more aligned with your principles. In the world of politics, this is why hot-button issues remain divisive even after events where one side of the argument is clearly in the wrong. The people who believe in a certain side of an argument will usually go out of their way (even out of the argument altogether) to find supporting evidence to defend their position.

The same phenomenon takes place in the office, especially with deeply ingrained matters like organizational culture, business model, and workplace policies. The veteran employees will often resist all possible attempts to change these aspects (however dated) at all costs. The same goes for business ideas and project management. Once a person takes one side of the argument, the ego drives them to dig in their heels and defend their position at all costs. It is a highly confrontational issue that could destroy not only the team spirit but also the efficiency and the ability to make money.

Selective perception exists in two different states—perceptual vigilance and perceptual defense. In perceptual vigilance, people will identify information that is contrary to their beliefs in any format that the information exists. Such people are likely to see opposition to their views, even where there is none. On the opposite side, we have a defensive perception, which focuses on keeping opposing opinions out.

So if a study is to be conducted to find out if the market is receptive to a certain product that someone is really invested in, the person with selective perception will scour the document to prove that a market exists. On the other hand, a person with a defensive perception will block out any information that seems to invalidate their view. Even more tellingly, people are willing to lower or raise the bar on the observations they make out of a situation just to validate their opinions.

Selective perception is formed based on a person's previous experiences, their attitudes, conditioning, age, and emotional state. People in similar categories among these demographics tend to have the same or similar selective perceptions about issues. As the leader, it is your job to learn how selective perception works and work as hard as possible to eliminate it from your own reasoning. This is accomplished by stepping back from your own views when assessing every piece of information and objectively evaluating the truth (or lack thereof) behind them.

Only when you have overcome all selective perception within yourself can you go to the next step of ensuring that the information you get from your employees is not warped either. You can do this by listening keenly to them and asking pointed questions to verify the source of their ideas and opinions. Only by resolving all disagreements on opinion can you then establish a work environment that is conducive to productive work. And when coming to a consensus, settling a point of contradiction with the resolution that you "agree to disagree" should never be considered to be a solution.

Ideology

In the world of philosophy, ideology is used to refer to a set of beliefs that a person holds. These beliefs close your mind up to other views, especially those opposed to your way of thinking. Every other piece of information that comes into our brains after we have formed an opinion about something tends to be examined through our opinions by accepting similar views and rejecting contrarian ones. On the other hand, business ideology represents the basic principles of a business, including the mission statement, code of ethics, and philosophies. All the decisions and actions that a business makes are meant to further the business ideology.

As a leader, you need to understand the ideology of your company so that you can work toward furthering it at the workplace. But you can also take it a step further and create your own ideology as part of your personal brand. Creating and working according to your personal ideology within the company will allow you to stand out from your peers in a huge way. There are also other ways for you as a leader to deal with business ideologies at the workplace.

When hiring, you should always ensure that the new employee exemplifies the business ideologies you are supposed to advance as a leader. The suitability of an employee to a position is best decided through ideological examination. After they have passed the ideological test, you can be assured that they will fit in the workplace just fine. Employees whose professional values are aligned with those of their employer have been proven to perform better and further the objectives more than those who are distinctly different.

The second way for a leader to deal with ideologies at the workplace is to be an example to other employees. The actions of a leader will always be scrutinized more than their words, so if you speak a big game but your actions do not reflect it, you will have a discordant group of followers. However, reflecting the values that you advocate will unite your team and make a more effective workplace culture. When making everyday decisions, you should consult your professional ideology and business philosophy. Just be careful not to make these beliefs into blinders that will cause you to have selective perception and confirmation bias. The ability to interpret all information objectively cannot be overstated.

Finally, as a leader, you are expected to be the ultimate authority on ideologies at the workplace. You should correct errors resulting from actions that are not based on the business ideology whenever and wherever they occur. Ideological differences are not the kind of discrepancies that you should wait to address during performance meetings. The cost to the business culture will be too great if errors are not fixed immediately and with conviction.

As much as ideologies prejudice people to discordant views, nothing unites people as much as a commonly held ideology. As a business leader, you should create an ideology for the workplace and ensure that your team adheres to it. The harmony that will result from this simple action will surprise you with how much it ties your team together and allows your team to work as a front toward a common goal.

Stoicism for Business

Among the most successful businessmen of this age, a common personality trait called Stoicism is very popular. It is a philosophy founded by Marcus Aurelius, an old Roman businessman who lost his treasure at sea and inspired generations of conquerors and super-achievers by his handling of that misfortune. Stoicism is a philosophy founded on self-control and resilience—the two most difficult values to observe as a man yet the most important of all if you are to live a life of purpose.

Stoicism has been adopted by the best business minds in the world today, including the likes of Warren Buffet, Charlie Munger, Bill Gates, and Elon Musk, among others. In fact, the concept of Stoicism is what appears to link all billionaires together despite the path they took to arrive at their fortune. Whenever any successful businessman talks about the path they took to get to their most successful stage in life, they will always emphasize personal grit, self-control, and perseverance. This is explained by the fact that business is tough and demanding. It requires a great sacrifice from anyone who attempts to the greatest heights.

The central tenet of Stoicism is that we must accept our mortality to live accomplished lives. The reason why Charlie Munger and other billionaires advocate thinking along the lines of mortality and death is that they had to overcome one common failing among us "mere mortals" to succeed. It is the proclivity to waste time and let other people waste our time with unimportant issues when that time would be better spent pursuing our goals. People are usually more selfish with their material possessions than their time, which is the exact opposite of what Stoicism preaches. The one thing we have in scarcity, according to Stoic Seneca, is time. At an unknown time in the future, each one of us will encounter death. Because that time could come any second in the future, you ought to live every minute like it is your last.

Today, you will often hear people use the phrase "What would you do if you learned that you had cancer and you would die in one year [or a month]?" People often hold off thinking about the things they want to accomplish until they get that terminal diagnosis. Others simply waste away, accomplishing nothing of what they set out to do because they failed to pursue their dreams. It seems like only the most successful businessmen appreciate their mortality and make the appropriate arrangements to ensure that their time here on earth is as fruitful as possible.

After a near-death experience while vacationing in Brazil back in 2001, Elon Musk laughed the matter off with the words: "I guess I learned my lesson now—vacationing will kill you." They were words said in jest, but they give you a very clear impression of his ideas about work and death. One is inevitable, and the other is a choice. Work does not invalidate death, but a death suffered without accomplishing all you set out to do definitely invalidates life.

Steve Jobs is another Stoic billionaire. He made a very poignant speech shortly before he passed away in 2011. In a commencement speech at Stanford University, he postulated that our time on earth is limited and that each one of us has a purpose. Rather than spend all our time trapped in dogma or another person's life, we should follow our heart and instinct and stop at nothing to accomplish our life's purpose. Of course, the first thing to do on that journey is to find a purpose and commit 100% to its attainment.

If nothing else, anyone hoping to succeed in management and leadership should adopt Stoicism because every successful man and woman that ever lived have observed it. Think about it. Can you name a single hero who did not go through tribulations or one who did not exhibit a superhuman amount of self-control? I will wager you anything that you will not find a single person to fit that description. Even if they did not confess to being Stoics, they observed the principles of this age-old philosophy. Therefore, if you want to become successful, living according to the principles of Stoicism will already have taken you further than any amount of hard work ever could because Stoicism will first require that you discover your life's purpose. But for the purposes of this book, the following qualities are associated with Stoics in business.

First, you must be authentic. To become a Stoic, you must embrace each and every one of your quirks and view your unique features as an asset rather than a liability or something to grow out of. Even if you have a role model or a mentor, you must be true to your real identity. Failure to do this results in a second-rate personality and mediocrity.

Second, you must always be rational and approach issues in a logical manner. You cannot be a Stoic if the negative mental models discussed above bias your thinking. And after taking care of the biases and prejudices that cloud your thinking, you can then take charge of your life by exercising self-control all the time. Remember, you cannot control/manage anything or anyone if you do not first control yourself.

The third principle of Stoicism has something to do with discovering your purpose in life. It entails engaging in purposeful action at all times. With your purpose in life clearly embedded in your mind, you can engage in ten different activities that all tie together in contributing to the attainment of a life goal. As you start working as a junior manager, you must discover your purpose in that position, write it down, and work every day to achieve that goal.

Emotional Intelligence in Business

Emotions affect many of the decisions we make. Even the decisions we think were informed by unquestionable logic and facts are usually influenced in some way by emotions. They are all around us. They control us. In most instances, they run our lives. That is why marketers rarely ever attempt to appeal to our logic when selling us on something. No, they go straight to our emotions, and soon enough, they have turned us into the ultimate consumers. While our emotions are an important part of our identity, they are also rather easy to manipulate. That is why emotional intelligence is such an important quality to cultivate.

Most remarkably, emotional intelligence, as measured by most companies before hiring, can be very critical to the remuneration and promotion process. On a higher level, emotional intelligence calls for us to get a stronger grasp on our ability to manage our own emotions as well as those of others. I use the term "stronger grasp" here to indicate that you can improve your handle on the emotions you feel every single day. This can be done the same way you improve your emotional intelligence (yes, it can be done)—through the disciplined practice of emotional training exercises like meditation. People with high emotional intelligence are considered better leaders because they possess some skills that others do not have, as discussed below.

Self-Awareness

Emotional intelligence is essentially the ability to understand one's emotions and the stimulus behind them. It also entails the interpretation of other people's emotions, which allows us to relate to other people. Emotions control our lives in very subtle ways. Every unexpected mood swing and every personality trait comes to us from some emotion or other. Being able to reach down to these emotions when soul-searching to understand exactly how they affect our behavior is an indispensable tool. It means that you are always aware of motives for different behavior not just in yourself but in other people too. The first step in finding a solution to a problem is to understand the underlying causes of that problem.

Moreover, self-aware people understand their limitations and their strengths. This kind of emotional balance and self-understanding comes in handy when you experience strong emotions like anger. People with high emotional intelligence are usually able to control their reactions to emotional stimuli. This, in turn, ensures that your emotions never have to interfere with your job, making you a reliable leader and effective manager.

Self-Regulation

Self-regulation is all about a person's ability to regulate their own emotions and act appropriately. It allows you to practice self-control, which in turn increases your personal accountability score. Successful leaders know that the first person you should conquer is yourself because you cannot take on the world while you are incapable of triumphing over your own personal issues. A person with high levels of self-control will not give in to compulsive habits like drunkenness and other self-sabotaging behaviors.

As a measure of emotional intelligence, self-regulation also measures your understanding of your own values and your own personal code of ethics. The things that you hold dear (e.g., truth and justice, fairness to all, and the pursuit of happiness) all fall under self-regulation. They form the red line across which you would never cross. In essence, they are the values that make you who you are.

Accountability, as mentioned above, is another important metric in self-regulation. The ability to take responsibility for good things and bad things is an important measure of emotional intelligence. If you blame others for things that go wrong around you or if you give others credit for the things you accomplished yourself, your emotional intelligence is sorely lacking.

Motivation

How driven are you? Do you want to spend your whole life in the bullpen? Or do you want to move into a managerial position and have your own office? Do you want to be a junior manager your whole career? Or do you dream of heading the whole company one day? The last is a dream only the boldest dare to dream, but whatever your aspiration, studies have proven that people work consistently better when they have a definite goal. The quality of work is also much better among people with big goals because they need to climb a higher distance than the rest. The level of your motivation counts toward your overall emotional intelligence score.

To be more motivated, first, you have to be doing something you love. It is advisable to write down a few reasons why you love your job to serve as your "why" and "where from." You can then set some goals to pursue as your "where to." If you hold yourself accountable and pursue your set goals, there is no reason why you should not achieve those goals, however high you set them.

Empathy

Empathy is the ability to put yourself in someone else's situation and experience an event from their perspective. Empathy is the highest level of care you can show someone. Even if you cannot really feel their pain or struggles, you at least try to relate. As a leader, empathy is critical to leading your team. The empathetic leaders are able to grow themselves and their teams. They constructively criticize those who need criticism to reach their potential, listen to those who need a sympathetic ear, and generally hold the team together. Studies have shown that while empathy requires that you go the extra mile to connect with your employees, the effort is well worth it. Empathetic managers enjoy significantly higher amounts of loyalty from their employees.

To grow your empathetic skills, you have to be adept at reading body language. People communicate loads using their bodies, and anyone who cares to pay attention could learn a whole lot from simply looking at them. Being able to read people from their body language is an important skill that comes in handy, whether you are being empathetic with an employee or measuring up a prospective partner in a negotiation. But with your newfound responsibilities and power, you will have to ask the odd employee (or your assistant if you get one) to work late nights from time to time. You could do it the old-fashioned way where you simply inform them, with the attitude that they can either follow through or look for another job. You can also respond to their emotions about having to work late and reassure them that you understand. That way, you will get more out of them and establish a rapport.

Decision-Making 101

Whenever someone else makes a decision that you are expected to enforce, the impulsive reaction is to criticize it as a bad decision. As a worker bee, you will spend a lot of your time criticizing your superiors for the decision they make. Your limited perspective on the bigger picture makes you walk around with the impression that you can make these big decisions better.

This is a common fallacy among thinkers. We all overestimate our decision-making capabilities and criticize everyone else. It is a common feature of the ego to inflate the view of self by playing our own skills up and underestimating other people. It is a fact of life that people only appreciate when they encounter the same situations that motivated the decisions they criticized. At the workplace, you will only understand why your work was not prioritized when you are promoted and start to encounter the complexities of running a company. Only then can you start to understand exactly where the priorities of the senior management lay in the strategic outlay of the company and realize that you were totally unequipped to make the very decisions you criticized.

Historically, even the most well-meaning business leaders have made the mistake of criticizing the decisions of others and blowing up their own decision-making capabilities. When he was starting Walt Disney Studios, Walt Disney established the most conducive workplace for his animators. He paid better than other companies, encouraged a spirit of informal camaraderie in the studios, and did not even require his workers to clock in their work hours. He thought it was the decision that made his company stay ahead of the park. In his reasoning, the decision to incentivize his employees with great working terms and the best pay in the industry was a proven winning strategy.

The rest of the animation industry maintained a more business-wise compensation and organization strategy. They paid standard wages and demanded a fixed number of hours' worth of work from their employees. There was no allowance for an "informal" atmosphere at Metro Goldwin Meyer or Universal Studios (the competitors of Walt Disney Studios) even though they produced cartoons like *Tom and Jerry* and *Oswald the Lucky Rabbit* respectively. The point is, despite being respectable companies producing iconic animated contents, Walt Disney looked down on them for the decision to treat their animation departments like any other department. He felt that his own decision to incentivize his employees with friendly terms of work was better than the rest of the industry.

In 1940, his workers were recruited into the newly formed Screen Cartoonist's Guild labor organization. It represented the workers from his competitors as well as his company. In a dispute that escalated with every passing day, his animators would end up striking and setting up a picket line in front of his studios in 1941. When he finally managed to negotiate a get-back-to-work deal, his company had gone almost a whole month with no one at the studios, and his debt situation (which had been bad before the strike) was approaching crisis levels.

Even though he had made the decision to treat his employees in a more informal manner to make their lives easier, his company suffered for it. In the end, he had to lay off almost half the workforce just to manage the wage bill his employees

49

had arm-twisted out of him. His great shock was the realization that after opening his bank accounts with more than generous salaries and increments, his employees were not likely to be more loyal. When he was done negotiating to end the strike and open the studio for business once more, he was so disgusted with the whole situation that he decided to take a vacation to South America for months.

Walt Disney was more formalized with the clocks, timesheets, and quotas that he had previously decided against and derided competing studios for enforcing. The decisions of his competitors to formalize the workplace were not looking so misinformed after all.

When you become a leader, you become a part of the corporate model of your company. The role you play from the moment you are awarded that promotion that entitles you to the title of manager is advancing the objectives and goals of the highest echelons of the company. As a common worker, you are responsible for implementing the action plans that have been deliberated on by your superiors as being the most suitable stratagem to achieve certain goals. When you become a leader, your thinking should shift from implementation to strategic thinking. You become a part of the company's central nervous system responsible for devising and implementing action plans. The most effective managers are those who familiarize themselves to the company ideology and action plan, then make plans to make it easier for it to come to being.

Chapter 3: The Thought Patterns of Successful Managers

Successful managers tend to think in a very similar way. If you study the thought patterns of the top 20 richest businessmen in the world, you will spot some very distinct similarities. Even though they come from different industries and follow distinct paths to their massive success, you can connect their thought patterns. The most successful men in the world have always been bold thinkers. If not in innovating new ways of doing things to make them more effective, they have created value by coming up with new systems. Some, like Einstein, took a leap of imagination, came up with scientific theories, and expanded humankind's understanding of the world we live in. Every aspiring leader needs to adopt this kind of bold thinking if they hope to achieve even a fraction of what the likes of Einstein, Steve Jobs, and Bill Gates, just to name a few, have achieved.

In this topic, we will focus on discovering the thought patterns that made the most successful managers successful. We will start with decision-making before moving to more sophisticated systems of thought, including the Bayesian concept and reverse thinking. We will illustrate how distinguished thinking leads to successful careers wherever one may decide to establish their career. To do this, we will rely heavily on the life stories of some of the most successful thought leaders in the world, including Ray Dalio, Elon Musk, and Albert Einstein.

Decision-Making 102

In your capacity as a manager, you will be required to answer hundreds of questions every day. You will also make numerous decisions with far-reaching impacts. Every decision you make as a manager will affect the employees you lead, the company you work for, and the customers you serve. You can no longer take decision-making lightly. At the same time, the sheer volume of decisions you will be asked to make calls for the ability to make great decisions in half the time. In "Decision-Making 101," we addressed the fallacious perceptions of decision-making that most people have in which they have a bloated idea of their ability to decide while disparaging other people's choices.

In this section, we will look at the exact strategies you can follow to improve your decision-making skills. What follows is a systematic master plan that will streamline your administrative functions and make you a better leader.

Systemizing

As much as you need to make them, the small decisions in life tend to have a very serious clattering effect on your brain. They drain your mental energies so that you cannot dedicate the entirety of your mind to the important things. From the analysis of the decision-making habits of great managers, you will realize that they eliminate these questions from the word go, freeing up their time to more important pursuits. The solution is to cut down the hundreds of small decisions you will be required to make every day to a few huge critical ones. In the study of systemizing, we will study the habits of the previous president of America Barrack Obama.

As the manager of the world's biggest economy, there was obviously a lot of demands on President Obama's time. The decisions he made would affect the whole world, so it was even more important that he made the right ones. By cutting down decisions like his wake-up time, morning routine, the clothes he would wear to the office (he only wore blue or gray), and the breakfast he ate, he was able to save on his mental energies on the hundreds of more important decisions he would make on a daily basis.

It may not seem like much, but a routine like this one can go a long way in improving your decision-making capabilities. When paired with the other strategies that we will discuss in this section, it will play a huge part in transforming you into the kind of manager you have always wanted to become.

Vision

If I could give you a strategy to improve your decision-making capabilities, I would use "vision." When you make decisions based on a clearly defined vision, you will cut down on a big chunk of discordant decisions that you will be asked to make. This is how it works:

As soon as you take up the managerial position, you sit down and draft a vision for yourself and the department. This vision should take into account the overall vision and mission statements of the company so that whatever vision you write will fit your job description. Be as detailed as possible about the different dreams and goals you hope to achieve. You can work within the time frames set by the company, or you can create your own. Be careful not to overestimate your abilities or underestimate the time needed to accomplish a particular objective. That is the worst rookie mistake you could ever make, and it might cause you untold problems.

Any time you are faced with a question or decision, you will have a very specific way of answering it. You will simply ask yourself, "Does the action that results from this decision align with my vision?" If it does not align, your decision is made for you; and if it does, you can then set about attempting to accomplish it.

Being Resolute

One of the worst things you can do as a leader is to walk back on your decision. It gives the impression that you are weak and unsure of yourself, which can, in turn, undermine your leadership. However, there is a difference between being resolute and being stubborn. Stubbornness is when you continue holding on to a belief even after it has been proven to be wrong. It endangers your team, vision, and career because you could be holding on to a wrong decision. Your superiors might not look very kindly at resoluteness if it ends up costing their company money. In fact, it is the definition of a *wise person* to be able to accept it when they make mistakes and work to correct them.

The way decision-making works is that if you make your decision right, you will not have to revise it for anything. Therefore, resoluteness is created in the backend of decisions. When you evaluate the data, take care of all loose ends, and consult with the experts to make a decision. You will have all the incentive to stick it out.

This is the difference between an unpopular decision and a wrong one. An unpopular decision will be validated in the end, so you should definitely stick it out despite initial opposition. Soon enough, you will be validated as a visionary. Some of the most successful businesses of today were once considered to be terrible ideas before they were proven to be visionary.

When Steve Jobs made the decision to start designing the Macintosh, he was determined to make it the best-selling personal computer in the market. The decision was so unpopular that he was fired from his own company. Today, Apple is the only company in the world to have reached a market capitalization of $1 trillion. The company has been able to reach these great heights by capitalizing on the Macintosh technology Steve Jobs had once been fired for pursuing. Talk about vilification!

In conclusion, the best way to make the hundreds of decisions that you, as the manager, usually have to make on a daily basis is not to do everything by yourself. When creating a vision, ensure that the employees understand the common goal and base their actions on it. You can then focus on strategic planning and supervision for greater success. This also means that your department works as a system rather than as an extension of you. When a system is in place and functioning well, you can usually take off without worrying that things will go wrong. It is when things start going awry as soon as you are out of the office that you should be concerned.

Mental Models for Systematized Decision-Making

When creating a systemized decision-making and thought process, we try to prioritize outcomes. The idea is to create a system that allows you to maximize outcome with minimal time and capital resources. Systemizing should follow the thinking process listed below:

In the first step of establishing a systemized decision-making organization, you reflect on the vision and mission of your company. This allows you to identify the work process that is involved in the accomplishment of various tasks. The outline of the work systems should be work centered; otherwise, you will just entangle yourself more in the process. Second, you come up with an objective statement, paying attention to the strengths, weaknesses, goals, and the strategies you think would make it possible to attain the goals. You can then make a general operating procedure made out of work procedures to accomplish the most common tasks around the workplace. The procedures should be sensible, practical, and simple for every employee to understand.

The third and final process in systemizing the decision-making procedure in the workplace is to ensure that you keep tweaking it. Constant updating will enable you to cut off redundant procedures, add new ones as needed, and keep everything perfectly up-to-date. When the system no longer serves its purpose of freeing you up from the hundreds of decisions you have to make daily, you must adjust. Studies have shown that highly successful people all put in place systems to help them save time in order to improve their personal performance. The Pareto principle applies to decision-making—meaning that 90% of the decisions we make apply to 10% of the most intense job activities we engage in at the workplace.

As for specific mental models, the best one to apply for decision-making is the Eisenhower matrix. Eisenhower was the supreme commander of the US forces in World War II and 34th president of the United States. He was a highly productive leader, achieving great things both in his military and political career. His life was organized using the four-part box matrix denoting activities that fell into different categories of urgency and importance.

The first box contains focus tasks. It contains the most urgent and most important tasks in your diary. These ones should be prioritized over all other tasks and be done as soon as possible. The importance of the tasks that fall here means that a leader ought to address them personally.

The second box is for your goals. The tasks that go here are very important but not urgent. You can set a future time to do them and carry on with the urgent for the meantime. Any good goals in this category move into the focus box as soon as they become urgent.

The third box of the Eisenhower matrix contains fit-in tasks. The tasks in this box are urgent but unimportant. You can get away with delegating them to your assistant or any other employee in your team.

Finally, we have the backburner box. It contains the tasks that are neither urgent nor important. They are mere distractions that you should eliminate so you can focus on tasks that are more important.

The problem with many managers is that they waste a lot of their energy and time on the third and fourth boxes instead of focusing on the first and second ones. As a result, their productivity suffers. The only decisions you should make are the ones in the important boxes. With proper insight and planning, you can also eliminate the urgency from your decision-making by focusing on the goals box. This is especially critical if you do not perform well under pressure.

The Common Mistakes of Beginning Leaders

The skillset that got you to the manager's office will not keep you there or take you to the next step in your career. For most managers, the first few months or years of their job is spent making mistakes and learning from them. However, if you know these mistakes going in, you can probably save yourself some trouble and propel your career to great heights right away. In this section, we shall look at some of the common mistakes that beginner leaders make that impede their progress as leaders. It is meant to be a guide for you to avoid repeating them.

1. *You try to prove to the whole office that you are the best.*

After a promotion, it is very common for the new manager to feel the need to validate themselves. This is especially common if you beat out some serious competition to clinch the office. As a result, most new managers will continue to perform their old technical job long into the managerial position. What they do not seem to understand is that management is a completely new ballgame. Your priority as a manager should be to support other technical workers and help them reach maximum potential. Continued performance of the old functions even when you are expected to do other things communicates to the senior managers that you are not very confident in your own abilities to manage. You waste so much time proving that you deserve the promotion that you bomb it.

2. *You go out of your way to show everybody that you are in control.*

The natural instinct for a newly promoted manager is to go around doing things that indicate to everyone that you are in charge. In this mistake, most new managers will veto good ideas because they did not come from them, stubbornly push their bad ideas on everyone, and generally make a nuisance of themselves. What they do not seem to understand is that everyone gets that they are the new boss. Not everyone agrees—in fact, most people will have a very passionate idea about who would have been a better candidate to promote in your place, but everyone is acutely aware that you are the new boss. When you go out of your way to show that you are in charge, you waste time and energy that could better be employed in creating a rapport with solid strategies and vision. In fact, the more you try to show your employees that you are in charge, the more resentment you will generate.

3. *You immediately embark on a mission to change everything overnight.*

Unless you are Jack Welch and you have complete control of your department, going about your new job as if your predecessor did everything wrong hurts your credibility. When you are just a small part of a system, you have to show some regard to the system. Anything else sends the message that you do not respect the efforts that went into setting it up, which is an indictment of every employee that worked on it before. If you want to bring some changes, a better strategy is to invite the team to suggest changes, combine them with your own ideas, and then gradually put them in place.

4. *You fail to establish a rapport with your team.*

When you go into a new job as the outsider manager, you will have to take the time to know your team so that you can work at earning their trust. When you are promoted in your current job, you will probably alienate other peers who felt they deserved the promotion just as much. In both instances, you will have to reach out to create a rapport. However gifted you might be, you cannot accomplish anything without a team to support you; the team is indispensable. A one-on-one sit-in with every member of your team is a great place to start. It allows you to measure everyone up to identify their strengths, weaknesses, and career aspirations. Knowing all this information comes in handy because these people will likely occupy key positions and come in handy in helping you achieve your master plan for the department.

5. *You take everyone at their word.*

Now that you are the manager, the common employee will start viewing you as the establishment. Even if you worked in the company before your promotion, your old friends would start acting differently around you. At least until your relationship adjusts back to its old level (if it ever does), expect to be "boss" and not "Ronnie" or "Rick." Being lied to is one thing that comes with the new territory of being boss. Therefore, you must listen with your eyes as well as your ears to avoid getting taken for a ride. Even if you are a straight shooter, chances are you were not 100% with your old boss either. There were some things that you kept from them, and you probably exaggerated the difficulty of getting a task done to get fairer terms too. In fact, you will probably have some fun as you watch people act in a way that you have always done, thinking that you are none the wiser. As long as it does not hurt anyone, you can let the small things slide, which is actually another mistake that new managers make.

6. *You expect too much from your employees.*

You have probably gotten to the position you are in now because you worked yourself to the bone, observing long hours and going out of your way for the job. The sooner you understand that not everyone has the same work ethic as you, the better it will be for you. Some people only work because they need to pay the bills; otherwise, they would not be seen within a mile of the office. Not everyone cares about impressing the boss or delivering the best work on every project. Some are perfectly content with simply finishing the project and not being fired. It falls on you to motivate them to care more about their work. You will get more out of your employees if you can find a way to get them to care about the work, not just the rewards.

7. You micromanage your employees.

Very few employees would have micromanagement among the list of the most endearing habits a manager could have. In most cases, employees feel that having someone even check their work is an insult. When you assign a task to an employee and then keep checking in on them, what you communicate is that you do not trust them enough to deliver. Good bosses leave their doors open to any employee who needs guidance on any part of the task, but they leave them to their own means for as much as possible. If you are the micromanaging kind of person, a better option is to establish checkpoints when handing out the assignment in the first place. This way, you can correct any mistakes that might appear early on instead of when the whole task has been completed.

8. You treat all employees the same way.

Fairness is a virtue worth having, but there is a difference between equality and equitability. Among the people you manage, you will have the highly motivated and dedicated, the highly talented but unmotivated, and the ones who only do enough to deserve their paycheck among many others. You cannot treat all these people the same way. The thing that makes one employee feel valued (e.g., asking how their night/weekend was) could make another feel like you are intruding on their privacy. For some employees, extra work means you believe in them and is an endorsement of their skills, but for others, it is a punishment. If you do not know the difference between these two types of employees, it will get very tough when you get the need to pass on some work to an employee. As far as fairness goes, this is the most important area of managing a group of employees. Getting this wrong could result in resentment that stretches far into the future.

9. *You do not lead by the coach's credo.*

The coach's credo is a mental model in which the leader takes the blame for the things that go wrong but attributes all success to the team. The coach's credo is the ultimate leadership mental model. It heaps all the responsibility on you when responsibility is especially hard to bear and demands heaps of grace to share the praise when the praise is sweetest. If you can live by the coach's credo, you will prove your credibility as a leader to the whole team beyond a shred of doubt.

Mental Models to Prevent Mistakes

The common mistakes that new managers make are avoidable simply by avoiding them, but the mistakes associated with decision-making are rather difficult to dodge. But in all due fairness, mistakes are unavoidable when you are trying to do something important. In fact, in a way, it is the mistakes that make you know that you are trying something worth trying. Many (if not all) of the most successful business managers have failed at one point in their career. It is the power to continue trying that sets them apart from everyone else.

The happy coincidence about mental models is that they can be used to multitask. For example, the mental models that you need to adopt to avoid the common mistakes of new managers listed above are far fewer than the mistakes they prevent. And when you apply mental models to any process of your job, the benefits stretch far beyond the tasks involved with that particular process. In this section, we will touch on the mental models of Bayesian thinking, lifelong learning, and reverse thinking as the ultimate mental models for new leaders who are intent on improving their decision-making capabilities as well as their job performance.

Bayesian Thinking

Every good decision-maker applies critical thinking to their decision-making process. It allows you to assess the issues at hand, scrutinize every option available, and choose the most suitable one. Bayesian thinking builds on this process by introducing the concept of probability to predict possible outcomes for every course of action. Formulated by Thomas Bayer, Bayesian thinking posits that no decision, strategy, or model is perfect in its current state. There is always room for improvement that comes from additional experimentation and improvement.

Bayesian thinking has been applied in military search-and-rescue operations and on the battlefield to come up with the best strategies to win a battle. Essentially, every event presents an opportunity to evaluate the effectiveness of the original strategy. Managers who use Bayesian mental models to make their decisions are not afraid to make changes when it proves to be flawed. In turn, the decision stops being a personal choice you made and takes on a life of its own. When a change is made, it is not an indictment on your decision-making capabilities. Instead, it is an improvement of the same. This is the core principle in Bayesian thinking: situations are always changing, and a decision made any time in the past will be inaccurate to some extent now and will require to be updated so that it reflects the reality.

Applying Bayesian thinking to your work as a new manager means that whenever you make a mistake, you can make a change without feeling like a total fraud. Studies have shown that the biggest impact on decision-making is the personal element whereby a person loses confidence in their ability to do something when a previous mistake is discovered. Doctors who are sued for malpractice are more likely to make a fatal mistake on the operating table because their confidence has been shaken. The same applies to managers. Normally, a previous decision that turns out to have been wrong makes you doubt yourself and either makes you make more bad decisions or stop making decisions altogether.

Bayesian principles applied in thinking makes you recognize the exact areas of your choice that did not work out. This is called fluidity, and it posits that any opinion or decision that is turned around by new information is better than the last. Of course, you have to be willing to acknowledge your mistakes and assimilate new evidence for it to work. There is nothing to be ashamed about in a bad decision when you are willing to pivot. In fact, a bad decision has led to better things down the road.

When he was starting out with SpaceX, Elon Musk decided that the best strategy to get into the space rocket business was to use old capsules from the Russian space program to make his own. He tried numerous times to purchase these old capsules but failed every time. Instead of giving up and writing it off as a bad idea, Musk instead came back home and decided that he would make his rockets himself. This decision again appeared to have been wrong when more than ten of the first rockets he launched failed. One of these failed rocket launches crashed with millions worth of equipment belonging to the National Aeronautics and Space Administration (NASA) international space center. All through these bad decisions, Elon went back to the drawing board and adjusted until he finally got it right.

Reverse Thinking

Reverse thinking is a creative method of brainstorming that you can use to bring some fun in your team. Usually, brainstorming calls for participants to wrack their brains for the best possible strategy to do something. The increased pressure often makes it even harder for people to think. With reverse thinking, you turn thinking around and start with the worst possible ideas to accomplish something. You will realize that most people come up with ideas that are more creative when thinking in the negative. You then work backward from there to formulate a strategy to accomplish an objective.

Reverse thinking is also great for coming up with a worst-case scenario to help you focus on the goals you set. When used in this way, reverse thinking taps into another mental model known as *loss aversion* to motivate us into action. Loss aversion states that the emotions associated with losing are usually twice as great as those associated with gain are. In a similar style, the prospect of losing something motivates us to work harder than the hope of achieving something.

As a manager, you can use reverse thinking and loss aversion to make decisions by comparing the cost of not doing anything. Usually, the decision with the biggest opportunity costs also has the highest rewards. When you do not know what path to take, what better way to move forward than to think of the path you do not want to take?

Even more encouragingly, reverse thinking has been listed by Charlie Munger as one of the mental models he uses to find investment and run Berkshire Hathaway in his book *Poor Charlie's Almanac*. The reason why Charlie Munger uses reverse thinking is that it plays into loss aversion, which in turn affects stock investing in a massive way. Many novice investors have fallen victim to the negative effects of loss aversion. Some have sold their stocks at a loss when a little patience could have gone a long way in increasing their profitability. Others sell their most profitable stocks for fear of making a loss even when market trends indicate higher prices are yet to come. The worst are investors who hold on to loss-making shares past the make-sense price levels because they don't want to suffer a loss and would rather wait for the stock price to rise before selling. In the end, they usually end up losing even more money.

The same conundrum exists in the decision-making processes of managers. With every decision you make, there is the possibility of adverse events. If you are to take the time to consider all options, you could end up frozen and unable to make a decision. However, as soon as you start reverse assessing your options, the options will become clearer and, ultimately, easier to take.

Lifelong Learning

The concept of lifelong learning is as simple as it sounds. It states that we learn something new from every new encounter. Whether you make a mistake or you do something right, you can use this to make yourself a better manager by recording every part of your engagements. You will learn what to do from the triumphs and what not to do from failures. By adopting the mental model of lifelong learning, you take the sting out of losing and enjoy your wins a little more as you learn from both. Lifelong learning also means that you should read widely and endeavor to expand your knowledge base with lessons from those who have succeeded where you intend to venture.

Story Time

To emphasize the lessons learned in this chapter, we shall look at the failure to success stories of Elon Musk, Albert Einstein, and Ray Dalio.

The Story of Elon Musk

Elon Musk is one of the most outstanding CEOs in the world. He is currently valued at over $20 billion, with two of his companies Tesla and SpaceX being some of the most popular companies in the world. But Elon Musk has come a long way to be the man he is today. When he was starting out, he was a shy young man who could not even summon the courage to follow up on a failed job application he had sent to Netscape when Internet companies were hiring everyone back in 1995.

He could have decided to take it in stride and go ahead to search for another job in a more relevant industry, but Elon Musk decided to learn a different lesson from his failure. He developed a mental model of looking at failure as a motivational tool and embraced it as part of the growth process. The change in mental models converted him from employee to entrepreneur and employer.

As soon as he had changed his mental model, the pathways to success opened up to him in a great way. Instead of seeking a job in the Internet industry, Musk instead collaborated with his brother to start his own Internet company that they called Zip2. Being a founding member, Elon Musk worked as CEO in Zip2 until the board of directors ousted him.

Throughout his career, Elon Musk has encountered numerous failures. He has overcome them all because he understood that failure is not the end of the road. Even with his most successful companies, SpaceX and Tesla, Elon Musk has encountered numerous failures. But his mental model has always been that failure is part of the innovation process. Once he accepted failure as part of his journey in 1995, Musk has achieved more success than most men his age. For his courage in changing his mental model from his very first failure, Elon Musk became the ultimate definition of trial by fire, of turning lemons into lemonade, and of persevering through failure.

In his countless appearances on interviews on SpaceX and Tesla, Musk has given the world a great look into his thinking. He has indicated that his genius lay not in what he thinks but in the way that he does his thinking. Thinking, Musk believes, has been influenced way too much by conventional principles and our inclination to draw parallels to previous experiences. He advocates a manner of thinking that is bound only by the first principles, which means original thinking that is unimpeded by the ideas of the world around you concerning what is right and what is wrong.

Rather than starting an idea by intuition, Musk starts by finding out the truth about a subject. This way, personal bias and shortcomings in knowledge are avoided, and we get the most factual model of a subject. When he was starting his space company and he needed to build rockets, Musk first identified the physics associated with space flight. He taught himself the whole subject of basic rocket science. He discovered that the materials for rockets made up less than 5% of the total cost of rockets. The technology took not more than 10%, yet rocket travel had been made so expensive that it was virtually unexplored. This is the kind of first principles thinking that we are talking about. See, most people look at the space exploration programs at face value. Only the richest governments run them because they need so much capital investment. Any accidents (which are common) can be catastrophic to the business. So why even bother considering it? No one has tried that anyway—until Elon Musk discovered that he could make a rocket at less than 20% the cost of conventional rockets.

From this point on, his idea stopped being bizarre and became a genius concept of exploiting an opportunity that has been right in front of the world the whole time. The government never had any intention of space shuttles. In fact, the whole space program had been started as a measure of wills and macho between the United States and the USSR. No more advancement had been made in the last two decades. By daring to observe the world using first principles, he identified a massive opportunity that everyone else missed.

The same is true for the battery parks that have kept the auto industry from moving into the electric space for almost a whole century. When he applies his first principles thinking mental model to battery parks, he discovered that he could take the price down from $600 per kilowatt-hour to about $80. This is a level that can be commercialized, which is what he did when he started Tesla. He has a very specific way of thinking that questions everything, accepts only basic verifiable truths as fact, and results in billion-dollar enterprises.

And in hindsight, even though it is not recorded anywhere, it is very telling that Elon Musk formed an Internet-based company immediately after being rejected at Netscape. After being rejected because he lacked the skill set the company demanded, he went to the basic principles of the matter. It was during a huge Internet bubble, so it was extremely easy to succeed with an Internet bubble. If he handled the management part of the company, it would not matter that he was not a trained programmer. When he finally sold the shares to Zip2, he made a neat $22 million.

The Story of Albert Einstein

Thought experiments are meant to challenge the thinker to consider a concept or hypothesis deep and hard. With thought experiments, you come up with conjectures, and without even meaning to, you modify paradigms for no other reason than give a sensible answer to an insensible question or riddle.

One of the most popular thought experiments is the impossible barber: If a barber in a small town cuts the hair of all the people who do not cut their own hair and does not cut the hair of those who cut hair themselves, who cuts his hair?

This thought experiment makes you think, but regardless of how much you think, there will always be a loophole because of the way the question is framed. No answer can be definite, and questions will always be arising.

The existence of the world is one such question. Scientists have been asking about the origins of the earth from time immemorial. Starting with a simple experiment on a beam of light for a children's book, Albert Einstein attempted to follow a beam of light. Instead, his experiment led him to form the theory of relativity and propel scientific inquiry into the origins of the world into a new age of empowerment.

The Story of Ray Dalio

The story of Ray Dalio is that of intense thinking on the subject of problem-solving. According to Ray, people have a tendency to tackle a problem at face value, which results in a vicious cycle of bad decisions in which one problem solved creates another one with even more dire consequences. This is called the first-order kind of thinking, whereby a person simply looks at the impact and not the consequences of their decision.

First-order decision-making is best exemplified by government-funded regime changes in other countries. The United States is responsible for creating some of the world's most dangerous terrorists when they fund separatist "moderate rebels" and arm them to aid them in removing a leader they don't want from power. After getting to power, these rebels turn around and establish an even worse condition for their people, prompting the cycle to be repeated all over again with ever more calamitous results.

From the school of thought of Ray Dalio, the only way to improve your decision-making abilities is to try to think of consequences to the <n>th order. Anyone can do first-order thinking, but only people with higher mental capabilities can take their thinking to the second, third, fourth, and beyond level. After taking your thinking to the next level, you can then follow through with the appropriate actions in full confidence that the consequences will be as you wish them to be. The levels of thinking are what people refer to when they talk about things like "two steps ahead." It means that you can predict what will happen when an event causes another to happen and use that to position yourself in the right position to profit. This is essentially what Ray Dalio has been doing all through his professional life. He has billions in personal wealth to show for it.

Chapter 4: Systemize for Productivity

The level of productivity at the workplace is determined in a huge way by the kind of management strategies used by the leaders. Decisions and thought processes are usually interlinked in a series of cause-and-effect connections. Therefore, the decisions you make on day one will still be relevant a year into your term as manager. As discussed in the previous chapter, decisions can be systemized to create a semi-autonomous working environment and free your mental faculties for the making of important decisions about strategy and direction. In this chapter, we will look at some of the principles that can be used to streamline the management process for any leader.

Systemizing Organization Processes

Half the things you will be doing in your job as manager will be organizational processes, otherwise referred to as soft bureaucracy. These tasks are critical to the survival of the organization because they establish chains of command, responsibility, and accountability. However, they also take up much of the time that you could otherwise use strategizing for new ways to do things and enforcing these strategies for the good of the company. Organization processes also tie you up at the place of work, making it so that you cannot be absent for more than a couple of days without a stack of documents pile up.

Successful managers like Elon Musk come up with such winning ideas and shine on a personal basis because they can usually take time off to think, strategize, and pursue apparently unworkable ideas. You can also do this by systemizing the organization processes that take up so much of a manager's time. With a system in place, you will finish all tasks in record time and leave yourself enough time to work on the vision you have created for the department.

Organizational restructuring is not that different from personal improvement. After all, organizations are made up of people with distinct values, worldviews, and mental models. When you decide to restructure the organization culture of a company, the first place you should look to is the personal beliefs of the employees who work there. In most cases, you will be surprised to find that the people working in a company have very similar characters.

Organizational restructuring is a big deal for any established company. It changes the way the company does business and, when implemented properly, is all but granted to act as a stimulus to better profitability. So when exactly is the right time to approach your bosses with a restructuring proposal? Below are the indicators you can look for in an organization to determine if it needs to be restructured.

1. **The old skills and qualifications of most employees do not meet the operational requirements of the business.** In a world that is constantly changing, skills are growing old fast. When you find that the business outsources functions for which people are employed to accomplish, then it would be a great idea to propose a restructuring.

2. **Communication channels no longer work.** Companies use performance appraisals to determine the effectiveness of the labor force in delivering the company goals. When the results of these appraisals are

warped or they do not reach the senior management in time, the company could end up getting stuck in the same underperforming situation year after year.

3. ***Technological innovations have produced a change in the production process in many businesses.*** Sometimes companies adopt game-changing technologies without changing the structure of the company to accommodate them. As a junior manager, it is your job to communicate with the managers about any changes you feel might be needed when a game-changing technology renders some jobs redundant or more staffers are needed to exploit new technology to the maximum.

4. ***The employee turnover rate is significantly high.*** When you see employees leaving a job, you should know that there are underlying issues that are not being addressed. When proposing a restructuring plan because of high turnover, try to find out why people decided to leave the company. In this case, restructuring should also involve a section on new ways to retain employees. After all, training new hires is one of the most expensive business processes.

The best mental model for organizational restructuring is the subtraction theory. Here, just like when it is applied to individuals, you endeavor to do away with all the negative qualities about the corporate culture in a group by introducing positive traits that you want to teach. And even though you will be tempted to keep ideas like these from your boss and instead try them out risk-free among the employees, the better idea is to leverage the people in positions of power. These are the decision-makers and policymakers, so convincing them about a point will result in better penetration of your ideas.

The policymakers are also in the best position to advice on the suitability of a model presented based on existing business policies.

Decisions Based on Numbers

There is a common saying that numbers never lie. Experts have designed numerous strategies of using data to make decisions, including probabilistic thinking and hypothetical projection. With hypothetical projection, you calculate the probability of an event happening and then formulate a list of possible scenarios that could result from a particular decision. The common feature among all data-based decision-making strategies is that they seek to eliminate the human factor. Instead of being in the driver's seat on the decision-making process, you are the conductor changing gears in a self-steering vehicle.

Studies have shown that executives are relying more and more on data to make big business decisions. Artificial intelligence and big data have created systems that make it easy for managers to delegate decision-making to data. While data should constitute a central part of your decision-making process, you should not rely on them to make decisions for you. The numbers are supposed to be an aid to the decision-making process, advising you on the most statistically sensible decision to make. However, the ultimate judgment should come from you. Because for all their accuracy and impartiality, numbers lack one very important ingredient that only a person can bring to the decision-making process—instinct.

Moreover, numbers are often deceptive. They do not always tell the whole story, and when they do, it is as good as the person reading them to put it together. Most managers will scan over data and look for the figures that jump out at them. This is called the bird's-eye view, and its main failing is that it does not give the complete picture. The alternative is to conduct a deep dive into the data and come up with insights based on critical analysis of the numbers. Few people have the right tools to do this credibly, which means that the bird's-eye view is used more than the deep-dive method.

The Minimum Viable Product (MVP)

The minimum viable product is a common product testing strategy that allows the creator to release an incomplete product to the market and rely on feedback to make improvements. Companies like Airbnb, Dropbox, Snapchat, and Uber all started as MVPs before being developed into the desirable products millions (if not billions) enjoy today. A minimum viable product serves the purposes listed below:

1. It helps you go from idea to market launch in a very short time. Usually, a product takes years and huge amounts of capital to develop. If you wait until everything is fixed to get customer feedback, you are gambling more than just the money spent on research and development.

2. MVP reduces the cost of implementing a product design. Even though it is offered in a crude and incomplete manner, an MVP will still be priced and marketed like any other product. This enables you to collect practical data on the willingness of people to pay for the product but also serves as a revenue stream for the company.

3. With an MVP, a company is also able to measure the demand for their product. This is especially important when the company offers an innovative product for which there is no precedent in the market. If the demand for the product proves to be sustainable during the testing process, the MVP will be developed into the complete product.

4. When you launch an MVP, you can send a team to correspond with the clients and hear straight from them what they would prefer to be added to the product after using it for a brief period. This is called sampling, and it is highly effective for gathering product data.

5. The main purpose of an MVP, however, is to prevent the loss of huge amounts of money for the company down the line. A new product is usually a very expensive endeavor, so taking chances is not something any wise manager would do. An MVP enables you to sleep easy during the final processes of creating a product because you finally know exactly how your customers will respond to the product when it launches.

Creating the perfect MVP is an art that few managers are able to master. It requires that you find the perfect balance between an overly burdened prototype and one with insufficient features. To be able to make a good MVP, you need to understand the needs fulfilled by the product such that you can narrow down to the bare minimum features that offer those needs with no frills.

The early or beta adopters will then give feedback on the features you have provided in the MVP, and you can add them into the product gradually. However, you must ensure that every feature you add increases the functionality of your product in solving the customers' problems. Finally, do not forget the golden rule of MVPs: feedback is everything. If your early adopters do not communicate with you about the good and bad of your product, then improvements will be hard to make.

System Thinking

This holistic analysis method caters to the ways through which parts of a system interrelate and how systems perform as constituent parts of a larger system. The system's philosophy posits that the universe is made up of systems within systems within systems, with every system in turn containing a series of smaller systems within it. This sort of thinking can be very conducive to the mental models that promote growth in the workplace. Systems thinking brings about some very insightful mental models, as discussed below:

Bottlenecks

Bottlenecks are described by the theory of constraints, which states that every system usually has a single constraint that holds it back more than any other restriction. In most cases, a constraint exists at the point in the system where there exist massive congestion and delay. But the most relevant thing about a bottleneck is that the whole system can only be as good as the worst constraint within it. They tend to slow everything down—meaning, that the system will not be exploited to its full capacity. To improve an inefficient system, you must identify the bottleneck in it and improve it.

Leveraging

When you understand a system, you can usually influence it in a big way with very little effort. This is called leveraging. It entails applying your energy toward influencing a system at the highest level of efficiency. In leveraging, you can create the greatest impact in a system by mastering a specific area to focus on rather than distributing your energies to a number of different sections.

The Feedback Loop

The concept of feedback loops borrows from the biological concept of homeostasis. In essence, it states that the output of a system either inhibits or amplifies it, but the opposite reaction happens to keep the system at equilibrium. For example, when a normally functioning body experiences temperature rises, the blood vessels dilate, and the sweat glands open up and help the body to release excess heat, returning the body to normal temperatures. When the body temperature drops, the blood vessels tighten, causing the body to shiver, generating heat and taking us back to normal body temperatures all over again. This type of feedback loop is called a balancing feedback loop. In the end, the system is left in equilibrium.

The second type of feedback loop is called a reinforcing feedback loop. It tends to bring about the deterioration of a system. On the negative, reinforcing feedback loops mean that when you don't fix an issue when it is still small enough, you will end up having to fix a much bigger problem. As a positive force, the reinforcing feedback loop makes viral marketing possible. Interesting and shareable content will spread faster through social media networks because increasingly more people share it.

Feedback loops also exist in our personal lives. Those behaviors that we find desirable are propped using balancing feedback loops. They consist of our bodies, relationships, values, the environment around us, and culture. When we fail to maintain these systems properly, they could turn into vicious reinforcing feedback loops. On the other hand, we can improve our feedback loops with heavy lift actions to create positive reinforcing feedback loops. Ambition is one such heavy-lift matter that can be injected into a person's life to make them more driven.

Pareto Principle (80/20 Rule)

Generally, the Pareto principle states that 80% of the effects come from 20% of the causes. Because the Pareto principle applies to every situation, it has come to be referred to as the rule of "Less is more" and the 80/20 rule, among other names. The Italian philosopher Federico Pareto, who observed that about 80% of the healthy pea pods in his garden came from just 20% of the pea plants, suggested the principle in the nineteenth century. He then went ahead and validated it by studying the land ownership system in Italy at the time. He noticed that about 20% of the citizens owned about 80% of the land. In the industry, 80% of goods in every market were made by 20% of the factories.

This concept remains as true today as it was more than one hundred years ago. You can vouch for this within your office: 80% of the sales made come from 20% of the salespeople, and 20% of your clientele generates 80% of the sales you make every year. Even from the wardrobe, we tend to gravitate toward the same 20% of our clothes 80% of the time. You use about 20% of the applications on your smartphone 80% of the time, and you probably spend 80% of your social time doing the same 20% of leisure activities. So just how exactly can you apply the Pareto principle in your position now for greater success?

You can decide to go with the flow of nature and identify the 20% of everything from your workplace. Find out 20% of your customers, 20% of the most important part of a project, and 20% of the most hardworking employees. You can then dedicate greater effort to understanding what makes the 20% such great performers and try to convert the underperforming 80% into high achievers too. There is one very important reason why implementing the Pareto principle at the office is such a great idea. You target 20% of your efforts on a goal and reap 80% of all rewards, which effectively means that you spend less time and less energy on fewer priorities for the maximum possible amount of gains.

One of the most common fallacies concerning the Pareto principle is that the percentage points in the equation must add up to 100%. This is not at all true. For example, if you decide to narrow it down, you will not get 10% of sales from 90% of the customers. It just does not work that way. In fact, at some point, it stops making sense that you are focusing your efforts on 20% of your market for 80% of the sales. Converting the 80% of the customers into 20% material might just blow up your sales figure after you have finished exploiting the 80/20 to the maximum.

Another common fallacy that arises out of the Pareto principle is that the other 80% is not important just because it accounts for such a small share of the outputs. This is false. In fact, studies have shown that completely ignoring the other 80% can have serious effects on the productivity of a system. As much as you should focus your efforts on the 20% to get to the 80% of outcomes, the other 80% and 20% of rewards are important as well. Neglecting them oftentimes leads to mistakes being made that imperil even the other 80%.

KISS Principle (Keep It Simple, Stupid)

The US Navy developed the KISS principle in the 1960s. The concept states that a majority of the systems are most effective when they are designed with simplicity in mind. Some of the best leaders in history use the KISS principle to cut through the noise and move past the debates, doubts, and arguments for and against an idea to get at the crux of the matter and come up with simple solutions that nonetheless solve the problem spectacularly.

The former general of the US Army Colin Powell is one proponent of the KISS principle. He recommends it for leaders as the one strategy through which they can cut through multiple choices and confusion to make important decisions in a compelling and transparent manner. Keeping it simple is definitely a great management strategy. Not only can you be firmer and more consistent with the decisions you make, but you can also display reliable leadership and integrity to your employees.

In project management, KISS principles tie teams together in their pursuit of project objectives because everything is communicated in a simple and uncluttered manner. It is much easier to focus on the priorities when all the priorities have been communicated in the simplest language, expressing simple goals. More importantly, simplicity reduces important points to the bare bones and ensures that workers are not bogged down in petty issues.

Negative Mental Models

Even before you move into the corner office as the department boss, you will probably already have a very good idea about the kind of boss you want to become. Popular culture has popularized the image of the reclusive boss who spends all his time at the office, has his finger on everything that goes on in the office, and pops Xanax by the armful every once in a while. Unfortunately, this picture is more often quite accurate.

If you are not very careful, you will slide into this self-destructive pattern in no time. We have discussed the mental models that allow you to build your managerial career with concepts and principles borrowed from some of the most successful businessmen and leaders in the world. But now it is time to show you the pitfalls that lie on your path to greatness. Borrowing from one of the mental models discussed in the previous chapter, we will look at these pitfalls in the reverse perspective.

Jack-of-All-Trades

It is very tempting to do everything when everything that happens around you reflects one way or another on you. As a leader, the outcomes of all members of your team will reflect one way or another on you. The senior managers will evaluate your performance as the manager of your division based on the division's output. If one team player bungles up, the whole team suffers, but you more than anyone else do because it is your job to ensure that everyone does their job well.

Managers often adopt the role of a jack-of-all-trades at the office, supervising everyone's work all through the work process because they feel their responsibilities as the leader in a huge way. Jack-of-all-trades managers interfere in their team's work and impose their own views on everything. But trying to do everything yourself does not make you a better manager; neither will you magically be able to multitask supervising everyone's work just because you are now the manager. The mentality that you need to keep your finger on everyone's progress to be an effective manager leads to working late nights and having dysfunctional lifestyles of typical managers discussed above.

Even if you can comfortably keep track of every department in your division or the work of every member in your team, there is no way you can do this and still have the time to lead. Some of the world's most successful managers run their multibillion-dollar empires from the comfort of their holiday homes. Richard Branson is one of the most hands-off managers, yet he is currently worth over $4 billion. I am not saying that you should be *that* hands-off, but it does pay to focus on one thing and trust your team to take care of their part of the bargain.

A manager who moonlights as the head of marketing, research and development, and customer relations will simply bring down the total output of these teams. First off, you cannot be as dedicated to these functions as the people who work there full-time. The fact that you are doing the same thing with other teams, fulfilling other functions at the office, also means that your focus is split. Not to mention the fact that everyone will probably be tempted to defer to your opinions on everything, which could be disastrous. So to put this in perspective, the only reason you should become a jack-of-all-trades manager is if you want to bring about the failure of every division in your department because that will definitely be the case if you involve yourself in every function at the office.

Perfectionism

There is nothing wrong with having high standards and expecting everything to be perfect. However, every rational-thinking person knows that perfection is a moving target that you will never hit. Likewise, perfectionism is a mental model that sadly attempts to attain the unattainable. In fact, perfectionism is associated with anxiety, depression, and in the worst-case scenario, suicide.

Perfectionism is not something that you should be proud of exhibiting. It is much healthier to be high achieving. High achievers aim for the highest rewards. However, they recognize that things won't always go their way, and they are okay with the occasional sub-par performance, as long as they feel that they have made efforts to achieve the best results possible.

It is especially impossible to do everything perfectly right after getting that promotion. In the first year or so, most of what you will be doing is getting acclimated with your new role and responsibilities. Until you have adapted to life in charge, you can then put in place the strategies to improve the performance of your division. Perfection, however, is a strategy that is fraught with impossible situations. For one, perfectionism is a very subjective concept. You cannot measure perfection, so it will always be a moving target. And while you might think that a moving target is good because it will keep you on your feet, just think about the anxiety you will feel from all that.

So instead of trying to do everything perfectly, you should set SMART goals and work toward the attainment of them instead. I am talking about the clichéd "specific, measurable, achievable, realistic, and timely." When you set a SMART objective, it enables you and your team to work toward a very clear objective. For example, you could aim at improving the work output of the whole team by 30% in the next quarter. This is both very simple and ticks off all the boxes in the

SMART acronym.

In their younger days, successful managers like Bill Gates set smart goals in their ascension to success. Elon Musk recently set a smart but bold decision to stop receiving a salary from Tesla until the company reaches $100-billion valuation in the next ten years. Smart goals are more motivating than the pursuit of perfection because they attach an objective goal that you can chase. While Musk tries to propel Tesla to $100-billion valuation in the next ten years so that he can get paid, you should set your own goals too. You do not have to make them so bold, but you should definitely challenge yourself.

Snap Decision-Making

We have been talking about decision-making from chapter 1. So by this time, you are probably fed up with hearing how much management is all about the decisions you make. But this issue cannot be overstated. Your legacy as a leader will boil down to the kind of decisions you make every day. And having discussed the right ways to make decisions, let's talk about bad decision-making for a while. Specifically, let us talk about snap decisions. Just for clarity, we are talking about deliberate decisions here, not the systemized ones discussed in chapter 3.

Snap decisions are those that you make rather spontaneously without thinking too much about them because "it feels right" or "there's nothing to think about there." These decisions can be very catastrophic, especially because they are likely to have far-reaching consequences that you did not take the time to consider. While there are quite a number of books advising you to make unconscious decisions because they are purer and your gut is always right, nothing could be further from the truth. Studies have shown that snap decisions are more than twice as likely to result in adverse situations that the decision-maker did not foresee.

Of course, this is bound to happen. When you make a snap decision, you compress hours' or days' worth of thinking into a few minutes—meaning, you do not have the time to consider all the angles. More importantly, the snap decision-making strategy goes against the principles of second-order thinking proposed and exemplified by Ray Dalio's mental models. With the limited time you have to make a snap decision, you are susceptible to numerous fallacies, including the value of information fallacy. This fallacy means that when you are under pressure to make a decision, otherwise irrelevant pieces of information carry more weight than they would have if you were not in a rush.

The final trigger to making a decision in such a scenario could be very irresponsible. In fact, people are more likely to make a snap decision because they are afraid of missing out. For example, you are being sold a great investment opportunity that expires in the next hour. The potential profits are out of this world, and you only have to commit to paying in writing for the deal to be yours. Later, you find out that the deal is highly risky or someone was divesting from a terrible investment.

Every decision worth making is a decision worth thinking very carefully about. Any opportunity that requires you to make a decision without thinking carefully about it is an opportunity you can and probably should do without.

Superman Complex

The superman complex mental model is a mindset in which a person carries an overblown sense of their own responsibilities over other people's affairs. It comes with the belief that other people are incapable of taking care of themselves or, in the case of the office situation, incapable of performing a task. When you have a superman complex, you will always be trying to do things yourself, and you will never ask or accept anyone's help. The main problem with a superman complex is that it deceives you into thinking that you are capable of doing it alone.

Another mental model that goes hand in hand with the superman complex is the martyr complex. While the former makes you feel an overblown sense of responsibility, the martyr complex gives you a saintly feel because you do so much to help others (even when they don't ask for your help) and shield them from responsibility. These two mental models are actually associated with responsibility deficit disorders, but instead of shunning responsibilities, you take on more of them than you should.

A superman complex is tiresome. Working at things alone because you do not want to ask for help is immensely tiring. The saying "Two heads are better than one" is universally popular for a reason; everyone needs the help of someone else. And when you are the manager, you don't even have to ask for help; you are entitled to the help of everyone in your department.

Another reason why you might feel the need to take on responsibilities that you do not need to is that you want very much to be the hero when things turn out great. This is actually one of the features of individuals with a superman complex. To remedy this particular impulse, you should train yourself to practice the coach's credo and actually give the credit that belongs to you to somebody else. It feels mighty good, believe me. And when things go wrong, you can take responsibility and even things out! (Hopefully, that will not be necessary.)

With bigger projects, you can go as far as collaborating with other departments to tackle them together for better results. Asking for help does not mean that you are weak; it means that you are strong enough to admit that you cannot do everything and that you are bold enough to ask for the help you need to improve your output.

Productivity = Time Worked

There is this common belief in management circles that you have to work long hours to be productive. In the 2015 Frankfurt Motor Show, BMW CEO Harald Krueger collapsed on stage while giving his presentation due to exhaustion. Studies have shown that while workers may benefit from working long hours (promotions are based largely on your job performance in your current job rather than your abilities to take on the new job), working too much as a manager could adversely hurt your health. Your value to the company as a manager is less about the number of hours you put at work and more about the kind of results that you can produce, regardless of how long you work.

As a leader, you need to be in the best state of mind (well-rested) to perform your duties, which includes reading and interpreting body language. Lack of sufficient rest also affects moods, making you easier to bait into arguments and verbal conflicts. This, in turn, creates a toxic workplace and brings productivity down. In fact, studies have consistently shown that overworking is a common trait among managers who aspire for outstanding productivity. While this would normally be a good thing, the implications turn sour when you consider that to achieve their inordinately high productivity levels, these managers pressure their employees into overworking too. The problem with overworking is that it does not quite work out. The most overworked employees are not necessarily the most productive.

Poor Work-Life Balance

Balancing your personal life and the office can get problematic when you are in a position of leadership. With technology, you can access your work files from any remote location, which means that you do not have to be at the office to be working. You could be vacationing in a sandy white beach and still be at work. This means that you do not really unplug from work. Your home life suffers, and so does your job in the end.

It is important that you maintain a good balance between your work life and home life. More importantly, never take the job home. And as much as the subconscious style of decision-making does not work on its own, the time you spend outside the office when you have a big decision coming up is a time you give your subconscious to mull the decision over for you. So as much as you need to hit the ground running and succeed spectacularly in your new job, take the time to exercise, meditate, and take care of you.

There are many reasons why you should take care of yourself first. The greatest of this is that without proper care, you will not be healthy enough to continue at that job that you are killing yourself over. And the worst thing about overworking and all the negative mental models is that when you are busy overworking yourself, what you are actually doing is sabotaging your own success. Former Apple CEO Steve Jobs spent thirty minutes every day meditating. He led Apple into becoming the largest company in the world by market valuation—an achievement that belongs to him more than anyone else, even though it happened after his tenure.

Poor Sleeping Habits

While it is not really a mental model, poor sleeping habits can be very detrimental to your ability to lead. Not getting enough sleep sets off a vicious cycle where you perform badly at work, get stressed about your poor performance, sleep badly, and so on and so forth. If you look at the lifestyles of the world's most successful leaders like Oprah, you will notice that they take their sleep very seriously.

The right amount of sleep every day (at least six, preferably eight) refreshes your mind, gives your body enough time to rest, and leaves you feeling energized. While you can manage to get by on 100-hour work weeks and little sleep for a while, you can maintain your productivity in the long run by giving your body the time to rest each and every day.

Burnout

When you do not give your mind and body time to recover from too much work, they often take the time out of their own volition. This is commonly known as burnout. This is a WHO-recognized condition that causes detachment from work and poor job performance. Too much pressure at the workplace is one of the leading causes of burnout. Feelings of hopelessness when goals are not met exacerbate burnout.

It is especially common for you to suffer burnout when you are working on a long-term project because the relief your mind gets after achieving a set goal just stretches into the distant future. When you combine insecurities about the risks associated with big projects, the pressure makes your mind very open to burnout. When working on a big long-term project, it is better to subdivide it into individual tasks and take the time out to celebrate the completion of every task.

Chapter 5: Negotiation—How to Make It a Win-Win

Negotiation is essentially a discussion conducted with the aim of reaching an agreement between two parties. In more technical terms, negotiation is what happens when both parties are mutually interested in reaching the agreement. For example, when one party is willing to sell and the other is looking to buy, that is a negotiation. With mutual interest established, all that remains is to reach an agreement on the terms of the agreement.

Negotiating is an art and science that only few business managers ever master. The ones who master negotiation thrive because they can always acquire what they need to pursue their goals while those who are incompetent negotiators will struggle to make headway in achieving their goals.

At one point in your managerial career, you will be asked to step up to the negotiation table and make a deal for the company. Negotiations are part of the running of a company. You will have to negotiate when you need to buy some proprietary software to streamline the business operations, when you hire a new employee, when you have to collaborate with business partners for any purpose, and in numerous other instances. It is very important, therefore, to understand and grasp the mental models of outstanding negotiators. In this chapter, we shall cover everything there is to know about negotiations.

Characteristics

Quid Pro Quo

Quid pro quo is a Latin term that means "something in exchange for something." The thing that you need from a negotiation is what guides your whole negotiation strategy, including the concessions you are willing to give. Just keeping in mind that the discussion is taking place because your negotiation partner needs something from you can help you keep everything in perspective. Quid pro quo is meant to reflect the values of fairness, but it can be used as a power tool just as easily.

When going into a negotiation, good negotiators assess the value of their concession against the rewards (what the other party is willing to give in return). The value both of you place on the things you are willing to give away to get what the other party has will determine the power dynamics of the negotiation. If your opponent senses that you are more desperate to reach a deal, they are likely to up their ante and take advantage. In the same vein, if either of the two parties is in negotiations with an interested third party, the probability of losing out if they go with the alternative deal shifts the power dynamics in their favor.

Same Interest

As much as your opponent will measure you up to determine your level of investment in the deal, the interests you share with them is one of the molding blocks of negotiations. Both of the parties in the negotiation table is usually looking to benefit by acquiring something the other party is willing to give. Your mutual and complementary interest with the other party connects you together. Whenever the interests of the parties involved mismatch, negotiations tend to go sideways. In fact, most negotiations fail because the two parties do not see eye to eye on their respective interests. If you are hunting for a willing partner to negotiate some sort of deal with, always look for one with whom your interests are aligned. Otherwise, you will be selling your deal to a disinterested party, which is much harder to do.

Compromise

Compromise is an important part of a negotiation. Even though you share the same or similar interests, most often than not, a deal will not be struck until one of the two parties or both are willing to give up or take less than they were hoping to get.

Reluctance

Especially in a persuasion, one party is usually an unwilling participant in the negotiation process. The reluctant party position is one of prestige because it falls on the other one to bring you to the table with a sweetened deal. A reluctant participant holds all the cards until the crafty negotiator arouses their interest with a dangled carrot and makes them want to negotiate.

Trade-Off

Every person in a negotiation gives something up. This is what makes it a negotiation; an exchange of some sort must take place. The trade-off is a characteristic of a successful negotiation. When a negotiation falls apart for whatever reasons, no trade-off takes place.

Mutual Benefit

The mutual benefit aspect of a negotiation is very important. The only reason why people enter into negotiations is that they want something the other gives, and they are willing to pay for it. The antithesis of mutual benefit in negotiation is the hostile takeover where an interested party foregoes pursuing a merger or acquisition and takes ownership of another business by buying out their shares and leveraging them to get what they want, usually a stake in a successful business.

Anchoring and Adjustment

When two parties start a negotiation, they both set parameters. If the parameters match, the negotiation could just be a handshake, and then the parties sign an agreement. Where they do not match, negotiators are anchored by the lowest or highest price past which they are not willing to go. Adjustments are then made to move closer to a mutually acceptable agreement.

Bargaining Zone

To illustrate this characteristic, let us look at a negotiation to buy a house. The seller quotes $500,000, and the buyer makes a counter-offer for $400,000. The gap between what the buyer is willing to pay and what the seller is willing to sell for is called the bargaining zone.

Negotiation Skills

As with anything else that you will do as a manager, it is always better to build your negotiation skills. And apart from building the confidence that allows you to charge into the boardroom and boldly ask for what you need, the following are some of the skills that are critical for effective negotiation.

Set Some Negotiation Goals

You know exactly what you are looking for in that deal; there is no doubt in your mind about that. But is it enough to know what you want? The answer is no. You have to be very clear about the goal and the concessions you are willing to give to get the thing you want. In setting the goals for the negotiation, you should consider the best-case scenario of the discussion, the bottom line, and the plan B. This way, you will have all your bases covered.

If you walk into that negotiation room and receive an offer that is within your range, you can take it right away, subject to a few considerations. Body language is one thing that you can read to determine if the person you are negotiating with is a straight shooter of the kind of person who enjoys a drawn-out haggling. If you accept the first offer of a haggler, they might take it as an offense and rescind. Haggling with a straight shooter when they have given you a fair deal is also a bad idea .

The bottom line is the lowest price you are willing to accept for something you are selling or the highest one that you can pay for something. This price point should be set based on data analysis and should never be violated.

Your plan B is what is referred to as the "best alternative to a negotiated agreement" (BATNA). Without a plan B, you could be forced to take a bad deal simply because you have no fallback plan.

One should have a *core negotiation strategy*. A negotiation strategy is like the viewfinder in a sniper rifle. You can try to shoot without it, but it is highly unlikely that you will hit anything. In a negotiation, you find the one thing about the matter at hand that the other person really cares about and use that as a bargaining chip. The core negotiation strategy allows you to get all over your opponents business and find their one weakness that you can focus on to get your way.

Elon Musk has managed billions of dollars' worth of tax concessions from the US government. He did this by selling government officials on the idea that his electric vehicles will not just spur innovation in the automobile industry but that they will also help combat carbon emissions and advance the war on global warming. The truth is that he would have made those vehicles even without the tax concessions. However, because he went in with a winning negotiation strategy, he managed to earn himself an enviable tax break.

Be in Touch with Your Negotiation Signature

Every one of us has our own distinct style of negotiating—from the people who give nothing to those who give everything, from negotiators who enjoy haggling to those whose first offer is the only offer, from people who go through the process of bargaining but are unable to close to those who can "close" anyone. It is all about understanding what you want and what the other person wants and finding the best way for both of you to come out of the discussion happy or at least satisfied with what they came out of the negotiation with.

Whatever your style of negotiation is, you will need to be completely aware so that you can measure yourself against your opponent. If you have no experience with negotiating and you are feeling nervous just before a big negotiation, you can practice with an employee or friend. As much as it is not the same environment, it will give you a bit of exposure so that you do not go in completely detached from your negotiation style.

Find Out the Reason the Other Side Wants a Deal

Negotiations are all about power, and there is no greater power than the power of knowledge. By looking carefully at what you bring to the table, you can try to work out exactly what your opponent wants from you. When negotiating with a professional, you may find that money is not the only motivation. Exposure is also part of the reason why a professional might be interested in scoring you as a client, or they could be using you to get to other clients associated with your company. Finding out information like this gives you an edge that you can use to haggle for better prices.

Play the Reluctant Party

In negotiations, just like in life, reluctance is a powerful tool. When you express reluctance about striking a deal, you force the other party to persuade you to come to the negotiation table. Persuasion gives you greater power over the opponent, which means that you can get concessions from them that you wouldn't receive in an even playground.

The first rule of negotiation is "Never show your weak spots." Eagerness is one of the worst vulnerabilities in a negotiation. It brings with it a measure of desperation, which can be exploited for a bigger share of the bargaining zone. So even when you need something, try as much as possible to come up with backup options so that you don't come to the bargaining zone with the least bit of eagerness.

In the real negotiation, your body language should communicate nonchalance and reluctance. This means that you should be relaxed, sitting back from the table, with no tension in your body whatsoever. This way, you will be communicating reluctance to the other side. If they are good, they might actually call you out on it. If not, you could make a deal at a fraction of the market price.

Mental Models of a Negotiation

The following are the mental models that the most successful managers use to get what they want.

Haggling Model

Everyone goes into a negotiation with a competitive mindset.

The aim of negotiating is usually to try to get a bigger share of the bargaining zone. Negotiations are usually very competitive, and haggling is the ring where negotiators square off against each other. In haggling, you can exploit a position of power to force the opponent to accept your terms, or you can exploit their interest in whatever you are selling for the same purpose. Whoever enjoys the power and the interest in the negotiation (or manages to convince the other that they hold these cards) always come out on top.

Cost-Benefit Analysis

You will be forced to make several decisions in the course of the negotiation about whether or not you want to take whatever deal has been negotiated at that point. Every time an offer is made, you must decide whether you will accept or reject it. The decision about taking an offer relies on the negotiation goals you set at the start of the negotiation process. Unless the deal on the table reaches the bare minimum, you should definitely not take it. However, if it is higher than your bare minimum but you still think you can milk your opponent for a few more concessions, you can make the decision to hold out, even if they insist that it is their best offer.

Partnership Negotiation Models

Negotiations are not always about seeking to advance your encroachment on the bargaining zone. Sometimes, the best deal is one where both parties meet halfway, enjoying greater benefits from a friendly alliance. Everyone in this model gives some and takes some. Some of the world's largest mergers have been made along the partnership model.

For example, in 2018 AT&T merged with Warner Bros to create Warner Media, allowing each company to consolidate their standing in their respective industries. From that partnership, the streaming service HBO Max was created to compete with Netflix, Amazon Prime, and other such services in the industry. From that deal, Warner Bros was able to capitalize on AT&T's large user base to compete in an industry that has been disrupted by new players Netflix and Amazon. AT&T's cable services also reaped the rewards of an extensive library like Warner Bros'.

Problem-Solving Models

Business operations are fraught with conflict. When the conflict reaches certain levels of escalation, the bottom line of both companies suffers. Sometimes people are forced to seek conciliation by negotiating with their business rivals, establishing clear-cut boundaries to de-escalate an otherwise disruptive conflict. Problem-solving negotiation models are ideal when both parties are hurting from a conflict. Even if you are the one instigating the talks, you will still be coming from a position of relative power because the other party also has vested interests in a cessation of differences.

When this is not possible, you can seek to strengthen your position in the conflict by negotiating with a different player. Even if you cede some ground to make the new deal possible, you will be in a better position to compete, probably even turn the tables on the original conflict to your favor.

In 2009, the Walt Disney Company acquired Marvel Entertainment in a deal valued at over $4 billion. The deal was negotiated at a time when both companies were facing massive competition in their respective fields. Marvel Studios was especially in need of reprieve from their main competitors DC Comics that had been gaining ground since Time Warner acquired them two decades previously. Having gone through a bankruptcy in the past decade, Marvel was in need of reprieve. Their problems were all solved when they folded under the protective custody of the Walt Disney Company. By capitalizing on the expansive distribution channels of Walt Disney affiliates like Buena Vista, the Marvel comic line has since had a resurgence that took them to the top of the box office just a decade later.

Common Mistakes of Beginning Negotiators

When starting out as a novice negotiator, business managers often make huge mistakes that cost them greatly. Losing a negotiation could end up costing your employer millions of possible revenue, and they will possibly not be very grateful. In fact, you are most likely to be reviewed or fired after dropping the ball on a negotiation you were entrusted with by your bosses. So to make sure that you don't make those mistakes that could put your career in jeopardy, below is a list of common mistakes to avoid when you are handling a negotiation.

Not Preparing Enough

You can never be too prepared, but you can definitely be underprepared to handle a negotiation. As noted above, negotiation is all about power and taking advantage of openings to encroach on the bargaining zone. To do this, you must perform all the necessary due-diligence studies to ensure that nothing surprises you during the negotiation phase.

Rigorous preparations also have another advantage. It makes you feel more confident going into the negotiation, which counts for more than just appearances in a negotiation. Sometimes even a partnership negotiation could turn predatory if the other party senses that you are ill-prepared to handle the talks. An undisclosed liability suit, a defective product that has been hurting the company's bottom line, contracts with competitors and partners restricting the business from engaging in certain activities—all these are worthwhile when you are walking into the negotiation room. Even if you expect mutual goodwill from the other party, preparing is 100% your prerogative.

Combativeness

Nothing hurts a negotiation worse than a warlike negotiator. In fact, the evidence points to the contrary. Agreeable negotiators sometimes make more headway in the negotiation table than the aggressors. Nelson Mandela is recognized by Harvard Business School as the world's best negotiator for his handling of the peace talks that abolished apartheid in South Africa. His negotiation style is described as amiable but firm. Without escalating the situation, he could push a point in a patient, practical, and strategic manner that left both parties satisfied that the best deal has been reached. In his negotiation for the lifting of apartheid, he made concessions that allowed the Afrikaans in South Africa to retain their holdings in the country—a contentions point that nevertheless allowed the country's economy to continue thriving.

Combativeness makes it harder to reach an agreement because it establishes a hostile atmosphere. People are less likely to concede a point they would concede in normal situations when they feel threatened. Furthermore, combativeness sacrifices rapport and common interest. It hardens the anchor points, making it that much harder to reach a deal.

Blindness to Options

In a liberal economy like the United States, your options start far before you walk into the room to negotiate. Whatever the gains you are looking for with one party, you can get the same from any variety of other options. You can create options by doing a BATNA study beforehand. And just because you have committed to negotiating does not mean that your only option is to make a deal. Sometimes, it is better to walk out of the room and away from the possible deal, especially if reaching a deal would mean breaching your bottom line. For the inexperienced, negotiations are taken to their bitter end, even if it means destroying any hope for a deal. Of course, you won't know this when you continue slugging it out with the other side past the sensible walk-away point.

From the moment you walk into the negotiation, you can calculate the possibility of reaching a deal by reading your opponents for the telltale signs that any experienced negotiator can read from a mile off. Does the negotiating team look open and willing to reach a deal; the facial cues and body language can tell you that. Are they eager, or do they look indifferent? Depending on what their bodies are saying, you can capitalize or adjust your strategy accordingly. And talking about walking out, did you know that sometimes walking out from the first negotiation saves the deal? Walking out means that you know exactly what you want, which often prompts the other side to revisit their options and come back with a better deal.

Underestimating the Opponent

Just because you come from a major corporation and you are facing off against a startup does not mean that the negotiation will be a walkover. Keep in mind that all successful businessmen of today started out as tiny startups. Jeff Bezos and Steve Jobs all started their multi-billion companies in garages, but they build them up through patience and resilience into the mighty conglomerates they are today.

The worst thing about underestimating the opponent is that you are more likely to make other mistakes like being underprepared and thinking that the other team does not have any option but to bow down to you. This could, in turn, lead to retaliatory bad faith, like the subcontractor who takes their skills to your competitor because you showed that you do not appreciate them. Remember, no matter how good of an opportunity your deal presents, emotions come into play more than any other factor in the making of decisions.

Caving in Quickly

Unless the person you are negotiating with send all the signals that they don't care to haggle, you should never deny the other party the chance to do it. Making a deal after haggling makes everyone feel like they walked away with a better deal, which is good for their peace of mind afterward. Let us say that you are negotiating with a real estate agency about leasing some space for a satellite office. You go in there and take the first deal they offer you and send the message that money is not an issue. They will possibly be left feeling like they did not ask for enough, and a few months later, they might be tempted to hike your rent payable. On the other hand, if you haggled hard and threatened to go to their competitor a few times, they will sign the documents with immense relief. After that, instead of sending you rent-hike letters, they will be sending you a Christmas card and going out of their way to ensure that the space is well maintained—what they should be doing anyway!

As preposterous as this concept sounds, it has been endorsed by some of the best scholars on business negotiations. If a product is negotiable, you should always start by offering less money. Even if you end up paying the asking price, the seller will feel that they deserve it more because they worked harder to clinch the deal.

Gloating

You have outdone yourself in the negotiation, and you have gotten a deal so sweet you feel like breaking into song on dance right there. Don't. Just do not. Gloating has the exact opposite effect to giving the other party a run for their money, only more intense. When we discussed the mental models of loss aversion, we established that people feel worse about the things they lose than the things they gain. When you gloat, you simply make your opponent feel bad about losing out to you. They will be sure to extract their pound of flesh should the opportunity ever arise.

Any wins on the negotiation table should be taken with grace and dignity. If your emotional intelligence is good enough, you will even give the other party a pat on the back for a battle well fought. Even though that will not assuage their feelings of loss, it will surely endear you to them. That rapport could come in handy sometime in the future.

The Psychological Insights of Negotiation

In his text *Influence: The Psychology of Persuasion,* Robert Cialdini discussed the results of his life-long study of the psychological insights of negotiations. His study resulted in a list of six principles of negotiation termed "weapons of influence." Anyone who is privy to these insights holds in their hands the power to influence the actions of others, whether it be in the negotiation table, at the office, or in the retail business. In this section, we will discuss these six principles in detail.

Reciprocation

Human beings are very transactional in nature. We all feel the irrepressible need to pay a good deed with another good deed. The principle of reciprocation transcends cultures, age groups, and social and economic classes. Reciprocation is deeply ingrained within us from years of evolution, so the impulse to give back when you receive something is virtually impossible to avoid. In fact, the temptation is to give back something whose value exceeds the value of the gift you received.

While negotiating, it is much easier to come to an agreement when one party makes the first gesture of conceding ground. Depending on how well balanced the other party is, they will either match the concession with another one of equal or greater value. This transaction is not just expected; it is often demanded. You will observe that when you are haggling, both parties tend to keep a close eye on the concession given by the other party. If you are buying something worth $100,000 and you quote a price of $80,000, the final price will either be $90,000 or within this range.

Commitment and Consistency

Caldini discusses the correlation between commitment and consistency. After paying the opportunity cost on a decision, we become almost irrevocably committed. Even if you were not sure about buying that house or hiring that questionable Fayetteville State University, you would feel more confident about your decision as soon as you have made the initial decision to do it. Satisfaction levels with decisions increase after the fact because consistency takes over.

After making the initial decision, your brain forces you to be consistent in your commitment to it as well as in making other decisions. A decision, even one that was flawed at the time, will often be followed by other decisions of similar nature simply because our brains are wired to behave in a consistent manner. So once you give some ground at the negotiation table, you are more likely to concede a few more points because your brain forces you to act in a consistent manner.

Social Proof

The most accurate way to describe social proof theory is that when in doubt, do what everyone else is doing. Caldini found that people were more likely to do something when other people were doing even when they were fundamentally against such behavior. He gives a great example of canned laughter in television sitcoms. Viewers and the artists behind the productions were unanimous in their repulsion to canned laughter, yet studies show that viewers laughed more and for longer when they were watching television programs with canned laughter.

Social proof is driven entirely by the deeply ingrained desire for us to fit in. When someone does something, we are forced to do the same even though we would never have done the same thing first. During negotiations where an impasse has stretched for a long time, the person who attempts to break it almost always wins because they take the position of leader, assuring the other party that it is okay to give ground.

Liking

Caldini's study found evidence that people are more willing to concede to someone they like than a total stranger. He also found that people tend to like people with some qualities more than others. Physically attractive people are thought of as being more honest, intelligent, kind, and talented, even when there is no evidence to support these assumptions. We also connect better with people who share our looks, values, or lifestyle. This has a calming and disarming effect, forcing us to look at the other person as a friend rather than whatever appropriate tag we ought to assign to them.

Outside the negotiation room, it is for the above reasons that salespeople are usually attractive, with generic clothes to avoid offending any sensibilities. A good salesperson will talk football with you as easily as they would talk 3-point shots with another person if they think it will endear them to you. Good negotiators know how to appeal to the interests of their opponents.

Authenticity

The philosophy of authenticity is based on authority. We are more likely to do things without considering the outcomes when we do not anticipate shouldering the responsibility of the consequences. In the study, when employees were reminded that they were not responsible for the mistakes they make under the instruction of their employer, they were more careless with their decision-making. This applies directly to negotiating. When you are just representing a third party, you should be careful not to make the mistake of careless decisions just because your employer would ultimately be responsible for it.

Scarcity

Finally, we have the theory of scarcity. Caldini found that people were willing to go out of their way to invest in shady deals just because they were harried in their decision with the warning that the opportunity would not be available for much longer. The fear of missing out (FOMO) comes into play here as well. Given a choice between getting something we don't really need or want now and the risk of never getting it (even if we want it in the future), most of us will choose the former.

In negotiations, you can normally get a person to agree to a deal just by taking it off the table. As soon as you do this, if previous observations are anything to go by, the other party will want it more and probably settle for less favorable terms than they could have gotten otherwise.

Persuasion

Even though persuasion is part of negotiation, there are times when the two are quite different. When one party is more invested, the negotiation occurs as more of a persuasion, whereby the interested tries to persuade the other into doing something they are not actively trying to do. For example, when you go to the board of directors with a proposal to fund a new product, you persuade them to see things your way.

The process of persuasion is relatively straightforward. Since you approach them, the tables are tilted in the other party's favor. They hold all the cards and may name whatever price they want, and you may have no option but to acquiesce to their demands. In the example given above, it is entirely up to you to convince the board that your idea is worth investing in. The decision to go along with your idea is entirely up to them (to a certain point). Even though the odds are stacked against you, it is still possible to get your way with an unwilling party.

The first thing you need to do is find something they really want. If you understand company policy and the long-term goals the senior management has set forth, the obvious way to win them to your side is to show how your proposal would help the company achieve these goals. You can then use framing to make the alternative (not going along with your deal) sound like a bigger opportunity cost. In another example, let us say you have identified a great opportunity to cross-market with another business in a complementary industry. You have to sell the deal to them by highlighting the benefits they stand to gain from it. It then becomes their prerogative (in part) to collaborate with you. Everyone has their price. As long as you can identify it, you can persuade anyone to do what you need them to do.

Conclusion

Mental models are systems of thought that affect the way we interact with the world around us. By using mental models, you can improve the way you manage time, apply your energies better for more efficiency in all areas of your life, and achieve success. This is possible because mental models, as used by the most successful businessmen in the world, constitute a higher order of thinking that challenges norms and encourages individuality.

Some of the most common mental models include success by subtraction, outlier algorithm, and the protégé effect. Success by subtraction posits that when we remove negative influences from around us, we are better able to achieve personal success in any area of life. The outlier algorithm sets apart and rewards unique thinkers by giving them the ability to spot opportunities that other people miss out on. Finally, the protégé effect postulates that people who endeavor to mentor others are more likely to succeed in life themselves. It implies that as we try to help others climb to greater heights, we are forced to climb even higher to continue guiding them.

However, before you can go about adopting new mental models, you must first search yourself to make sure that you are not the victim of decision-making bias. Even the most capable thinkers have been known to err in making decisions under the influence of confirmation bias, picking out specific information to digest. It is very critical for managers and leaders to understand how these biases affect their decisions because mistakes and poor decisions can have very serious implications.

Emotional intelligence is a very important building block for success. It prompts us to get a more profound sense of self through self-awareness, which in turn makes us more receptive to other people's emotions. With a better understanding of personal values, emotional intelligence builds our accountability and prompts us into a higher level of self-control. With accountability comes the push we give to ourselves to work even harder toward our goals. Thus, emotional intelligence builds on our passions and, having allowed us to get in touch with our deepest desires, fuels our motivation to pursue them. The most important element of emotional intelligence is empathy. It prompts us to relate to the emotions of other people, especially those we are responsible for leading.

Along with emotional intelligence, the most successful businessmen in the world also exhibit high levels of Stoic behavior. It is part of the mental model used by Elon Musk, Charlie Munger, and other highly successful businessmen. Stoicism allows leaders to persevere in the face of massive challenges. They also appreciate life, you can say, a little more than the rest of us because they have accepted their mortality. Stoicism calls for authenticity, rationality, critical thinking, and living a purpose-driven life.

Next, we discussed decision-making. The career of a manager comprises of a lot of decision-making exercises, with these decisions having a significantly greater weight because it affects the employees, the employer, and the customers. A systematized decision-making process has the effect of making life easier for any manager who practices it. Eliminating decision-making in small matters (e.g., what to wear and what to eat) has been found to free up our mental reserves to focus on decisions that are more important.

New managers make more mistakes in the early days of their

managerial careers than at any other time. Some of the most serious mistakes include flexing their muscles to prove to everyone that they are in control. This alienates team members and makes your job of leaders infinitely more difficult. Micromanaging is another serious and common mistake of new managers. Not only does it annoy the team members, but it also indicates an unwillingness to trust your team to deliver.

Systemizing is a strategy that has been used by business and political leaders to simplify their decision-making processes. In this, the concept of subtracting comes in very handy. It entails creating a well-defined vision for your department and ensuring that your every decision is made in service to that vision. To follow through, you should use the Eisenhower to classify your tasks into a matrix based on urgency and importance. You then focus on doing the urgent and important things and, if you must, delegate the rest.

When designing your systems, you should keep in mind that, by the Pareto principle, 80% of rewards come from 20% of the efforts. You should select the areas you want to focus on very carefully but not neglect the other 20% of rewards that come from 80% of the work. Another concept of creating systems is the KISS principle. It dictates that every system you create should be easy to use for any person and that your vision should be easily communicated and implemented. Some of the obstacles you will have to observe to create an efficient system include bottlenecks, feedback, and leverage. You should endeavor to remove bottlenecks, leverage on your advantages, and use feedback loops to motivate your team and yourself.

Another very popular mental model for systematized thinking is the Bayesian concept. In this concept, you use probabilistic thinking to predict the probability of a desired or undesired event from happening. It bears a close resemblance to the second-order thinking mental model that has been used by Ray Dalio to amass a fortune of over $18 billion. In second-order thinking, we are supposed to think beyond the immediate outcomes of the decisions we make. Failure to do this leads to a chain of events of ever-increasing calamitous impact.

Negotiations are central to a career in management. However little your experience in negotiation might be, at one point, you will have to step up and negotiate a deal for the department or the company. Negotiation requires a specific set of skills. Reciprocation is one such skill, and it can be both a friend and foe. When going against seasoned negotiators, you might get baited into an argument with concessions, conceding far beyond your bottom line. Another strategy used by negotiators is social proof, driving discussions into an impasse and then offering an icebreaker that unwitting victims are likely to fall for.

Being a reluctant party in the negotiation gives you a position of power, forcing the other party to persuade you to take the deal you wanted all along with better terms. The most commonly used strategy to close a negotiation when you hold power is to take the deal away, shocking the other party into a scarcity-induced acquiescence to your terms.

Negotiations in which you discuss a deal with an unwilling party are more like persuasion than anything else. At one point or another in your career, you will have to persuade someone to do something they are not necessarily eager to do. The secret to persuasion is to find the other party's price, then pay it.

References

Cialdini, R. B. (2007). *Influence: The psychology of persuasion.* New York: HarperCollins Publishers, Inc.

Levitin, D. (2014). *The organized mind: Thinking straight in the age of information overload.* New York: Dutton Penguin Random House.

Munger, C. (2005). *Poor Charlie's almanac.* Brookfield: The Donning Company.

www.ingramcontent.com/pod-product-compliance
Lightning Source LLC
Chambersburg PA
CBHW072041110526
44592CB00012B/1509